NIHONGO PERA PERA!

NIHONGO PERA PERA!

A User's Guide to
Japanese Onomatopoeia

Susan Millington

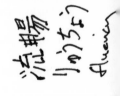

CHARLES E. TUTTLE COMPANY
Rutland, Vermont & Tokyo, Japan

Illustrations by Mitsuru Takahashi

Published by the Charles E. Tuttle Company, Inc.
of Rutland, Vermont & Tokyo, Japan
with editorial offices at
2-6 Suido 1-chome, Bunkyo-ku, Tokyo 112

LCC Card No. 93-60035
ISBN 0-8048-1890-8

First edition, 1993

Printed in Japan

· CONTENTS ·

CONTENTS

· PREFACE ·

I came to Japan for the first time 23 years ago as a newlywed, to begin married life in a country I knew almost nothing about. I made the journey by sea with my husband, a young British diplomat. It took us seven weeks to reach our destination. When I first learned I was going to Japan, I had no grand design on how to go about mastering Japanese, although the long sea journey meant I would have plenty of time for reading and study. Once on board the ship, I started to explore, in a leisurely fashion, what lay ahead of me. I scanned my blue and yellow *Teach Yourself Japanese* for days, confident I was making great progress. When we disembarked at Yokohoma, I had, in effect, mastered only two words of Japanese: *pen* and *inki*. I did not realize that *pen* really referred to something other than a fountain pen, whose correct name was *mannenhitsu*. Even the word *inki* let me down, as it is now more commonly pronounced and spelled *inku*.

We were to spend two years learning Japanese before my husband began work in the Embassy. There were three other young diplomats also embarking on language study. For the first time ever, another wife and I were to be allowed to participate in the training, with one proviso: our husbands and the other men had to be able to make satisfactory progress in spite of our presence.

Although I was not a diplomat, I would be learning the language of diplomacy: the vocabulary of politics and economics; official government jargon; *gyōsho* and *sōsho,* the cursive and very cursive styles of writing; polite ways to address the Emperor, should we ever meet him. It was very odd. After two years of intensive study, I could sort out a visa problem in Japanese or discuss a Ministry of Foreign Affairs *Note Verbale* with the loftiest of Japanese bureaucrats, but I could not have a casual chat in colloquial Japanese with my neighbor or simply and correctly order a bag of onions from the vegetable shop.

I remember how difficult it was to pick up the language at first. I had studied French, German, and Latin before coming to Japan, but nothing prepared me for learning Japanese. It is truly a difficult language to master, and many people must reach the conclusion early on that it isn't worth the bother. For those who feel this way about learning Japanese, I have four words of encouragement: First is the Worst. The stress of the first attempts to pick up the language is almost unbearable. Hairlines have been known to recede under such pressure, ulcers have formed, and romantic bonds have snapped. But it does get easier and, yes, it can be fun.

When I look back over my years of studying Japanese, I wish I had had more user-friendly materials to help improve my speaking ability. I've tried to write the sort of book that I would have liked to have had myself, a book that would have helped me improve my spoken Japanese and my understanding of the subtle nuances of the language. I've never stopped studying, but now I try to learn only what I want to know and what I can use. I have not had a chance to speak to the Emperor and have had little need to read cursive script. What I would like is to enrich my everyday spoken language and to use more effectively the language I have already acquired. There is no better way to do this than to add a few of the colorful onomatopoeic phrases the Japanese put to such skillful use themselves.

There is no right or wrong way to learn Japanese. After an initial period of hard work picking up the basics, it should become fun. Whether you are seriously studying Japanese, hoping one day to become a great expert, or just grazing on the surface of the language, trying to decide whether you want to delve deeper, I hope this book will be of use to you. Above all, as you read the book, I hope you will enjoy thinking about the language and how you can make use of these expressions yourself.

I would like to thank Keiko Plater for her assistance in proofreading this text and the staff of the Charles E. Tuttle Company for their editorial guidance.

· INTRODUCTION ·

If you have ever lived in Japan, you have undoubtedly come across the phrase *pera pera*, often used in praise and encouragment of any attempt foreigners make to communicate in Japanese. You've probably eaten *shabu shabu* in a Japanese restaurant. When you've barely met a deadline at work, you may have heard your boss mutter *"giri giri da."*

Strolling down a shopping street, you are likely to be struck by the noisy clatter, or *pachi pachi,* of millions of small steel balls coursing through the veins of Japanese pinball machines in pachinko parlors. If you get stuck in a traffic jam, you simmer with frustration at the slow driving pace, or *noro noro unten.* You are surprised when you discover that Japanese dogs go *wan wan* when they bark, rather than bowwow.

These expressions all belong to a very important group of words in Japanese, a group that defies our efforts to classify them. Are they adverbs or adjectives, sound effects or sound symbols? One scholar will call them sound symbolisms, another will carefully divide them into mimesis and onomatopoeia, with further differentiation between those words describing voices or sounds and those describing the condition of things or human emotions. None of this helps one to learn or appreciate the language, and the majority of Japanese themselves would probably have no idea what you were talking about if you tried to put these words in categories. However,

11

they would begin to relax immediately if you could skillfully insert one or two of them into your spoken Japanese.

Because I needed to call them something, I have gathered these words under one general heading: onomatopoeic phrases. The *Oxford English Dictionary* defines onomatopoeia as the formation of a name or word by an imitation of the sound associated with the thing or word designated. Alternatively, it can be a word imitating the sound of the thing or action that it signifies. It is a Greek word in origin, formed from *onoma*, meaning name, and *poiein*, to make or to coin. The great 19th century language scholar, Max Müller, described onomatopoeia as "name-poetry." Onomatopoeic words should express that which strikes our fancy about a thing, rather than the most important aspect or specific quality of the thing.

Japanese onomatopoeic phrases usually, but not always, consist of more than one word: be it the same word repeated again, such as *gota gota*, the same word repeated again in a slightly altered form, such as *dotabata*, or a word plus a particle, such as *kichin to*. Doubled words, such as *yama yama* (many mountains), are not included in this book. The doubling of a word is not, strictly speaking, a basis for classifying the resulting phrase as onomatopoeia.

There are many colorful onomatopoeic phrases in English, such as boogie-woogie, chitchat, dillydally, splish splash, la-di-da, hodge-podge, teeny weeny, and yakety-yak, just to mention a few. Sources for English onomatopoeia are much more practical, and not as poetic as those for the Japanese. As we have lived in proximity to livestock and domestic animals, words imitating their sounds abound in English. The Japanese, on the other hand, have many more words describing wild birds and insects, which they like to refer to in their poetry. In general, their language is rich in words expressing feeling; English in words of action. Japanese verbs are less varied, so they need to be described and explained further. While we plod, stroll, strut, and swagger in English, the Japanese can only walk if they don't make use of onomatopoeia to describe how that walk looks, sounds, or feels. There are few Japanese words describing taste or smell, but the Japanese are extremely sensitive to how things feel, and there are many onomatopoeic phrases to describe the touch or feel of something, even how food feels in the mouth. As in any language, there are many words and phrases to describe what is important to the speakers, or what sticks out in their perception of their environment. Anyone who has spent a humid summer in Japan will not be surprised to know that there are numerous ways of talking about dampness. Always concerned about their feelings, the Japanese have many words for expressing anger and only a few to express a calm state. These expressions are the music of their language. They bring poetry to their everyday encounters and transactions with their fellow countrymen, and bring life to the basic and monotonal speech patterns of their language.

The Origins of Japanese Onomatopoeia

The first noises a baby makes are only sounds, from which words later emerge. Man's earliest attempts at language must have consisted of grunts and cries of joy or pain or imitations of sounds in nature. When I decided to write this book, I was eager to discover how far back in time I could go and still find examples of onomatopoeic phrases in the Japanese language. If our earliest words were just sounds, it would follow that there would be examples of onomatopoeia in the earliest Japanese literature.

This was not as simple a task as it might seem, because the first form of writing used by the Japanese was Chinese in origin, rather like European scholars' use of Latin in ancient times. No trace exists of any writing system predating the introduction of Chinese texts to Japan around A.D. 400. Scholars can read these ancient texts, but it is impossible to know exactly how the language would have sounded when pronounced by the ancients. Eventually, the Japanese began to use Chinese characters phonetically, to represent individual syllables of Japanese names or words. The *Kojiki,* which appeared in 712, and the *Man'yōshū,* also compiled in the 8th century, were written in a mixture of styles, but are considered works of pure Japanese literature. References to the use of onomatopoeia in these two works are the earliest that I have found: *sawa sawa (Kojiki),* to describe a rustling sound; *hodoro hodoro (Man'yōshū),* for falling snow; *moyuru (Kojiki),* for rain falling; *koro koro (Kojiki),* for raking over salt; and *bishi bishi (Man'yōshū)*, for a sniffly nose. *Sawa sawa* still exists today, with its original meaning. *Hodoro hodoro* is no longer used but has become *hadare* or *hadara,* referring to specks or patches. *Moyuru* is no longer in common use but survives as *moya moya*, meaning foggy or misty, and is related to *moeru,* to burn or glow. *Koro koro,* now meaning to roll over and over, is widely used. *Bishi bishi* no longer refers to a sniffling nose but instead means to be strict or rigid, or to snap. The ancient phrase seems to have been transformed into the modern day *bisho bisho,* meaning dripping wet.

These very early literary examples of onomatopoeic phrases are not numerous, but this is because the sources are mainly songs or *tanka* poems of thirty-one syllables that were written according to a strict and lofty classical literary style. That they appear at all leads us to assume that they were undoubtedly numerous in the everyday conversations of the common people.

Japanese onomatopoeic phrases derive from three sources: first and most important, the native spoken language of the local people; second, Chinese words that were introduced into the

Japanese vocabulary many centuries ago; and third, words coming from European languages, such as *jigu zagu,* to describe a sewing machine stitch or a student demonstration, or *chiku taku,* to describe the sound of a clock. This last is the source of the fewest expressions.

When the rapid addition of words of Chinese origin into the native vocabulary began to occur, a method for incorporating them as adverbs had to be found. The simplest method was to add a particle like *to* or *ni.* Hence, we have *gō gō to,* rumblingly, *dō dō to,* majestically, and *ga ga to,* steeply rising, which date back to the *Heike Monogatari* of the 13th century. These phrases originating from Chinese are not nearly so numerous or generally so widely used as those that are purely Japanese.

Onomatopoeic phrases are widely used in news headlines because they pack so much punch in just one or two words. They also appear frequently in advertising, because they are catchy and appealing. Perhaps their greatest contribution to modern Japanese culture, though, is to be found in *manga*—the comic books read by young and old alike. These cartoons are littered with onomatopoeic phrases, enabling the artist to create certain moods without detailed description and giving the pictorial action a heightened sense of drama. Frequently, phrases are altered from their dictionary forms to suit the needs of the narrative, often leaving the reader to infer their meaning from the action. As a result of taking such liberties, sometimes the artist inadvertently coins an entirely new word that may gain a permanent place for itself in the language.

Note on the Onomatopoeic Phrases

In choosing phrases to include, I have tried to select those that are in frequent use. Rather than compiling an alphabetically listed dictionary, I have grouped the phrases into categories, giving definitions and examples of their usage and an occasional reminiscence on how I first came across the phrase. It is my hope that this will enable the reader to dip anywhere into the book and enjoy sections of it at random. In addition, for easy access, I have included an alphabetical listing of entries at the back of the book that includes the definition and page number for each entry.

Many phrases have more than one meaning. If a phrase is featured elsewhere in the text, an asterisk (*) is placed by the relevant definition. Check the listing of entries for the location of any other listings in the book. Different categories of meanings within each definition are separated by semicolons.

Most Japanese onomatopoeic phrases belong to a family of related expressions that repeat or pronounce the same word slightly differently, or add an article (e.g., *gun, gūn, gu-ūn, gun to,* and *gutto,* all describe with slightly different nuances, the use of effort, or marked change). Also, in *kana* the use of the *dakuten* (ʺ) or the *maru* (°) with the words can harden or soften the sound or meaning of a phrase (e.g., *zuke zuke* means to speak one's mind in a more direct way than *tsuke tsuke*). Wherever possible, I have grouped these related phrases together in the text. Generally:

g, z, d, and *b* are "muddy" sounds suggesting big, heavy, or dirty (like *gashitto,* strongly built, and *botteri,* large or fat)

k, s, t, and *h* are "clean" sounds, suggesting sharp, light, small, and pretty (*hakkiri,* clearly, and *soyo soyo,* light breeze)

h is a dignified sound (*hō hokekyo,* the call of the nightingale)

p suggests something undignified (*pota pota,* plop, and *paku paku,* gobble)

k and *t* are hard (*kochi kochi,* hard, and *tsun,* pointed)

s suggests a feeling of friction, of sliding or slipping along (*sarari,* slide)

n suggests a feeling of stickiness (*neba neba,* sticky)

16

h suggests lightness, *b* heaviness, *p* something in between (*hara hara,* water streams soundlessly, *bara bara,* rain down, and *para para,* sprinkle lightly)

When a word is repeated to form a phrase, it suggests repetition, continuation, or things happening one after another.

· 1 ·
WILDLIFE

In the City

I've always lived in Tokyo during our stays in Japan, and I've always found it a very noisy place. Tokyoites have grown accustomed to noise. During the Edo period, the cries of hawkers and shopkeepers eager to sell their wares filled the air. Now it's the sound of traffic and construction work that seem to be everywhere. As if that weren't enough, whenever there is an election, all the candidates dispatch cars with loudspeakers to patrol the streets, playing taped messages shouting their virtues shamelessly, until it's hard for me to understand why anyone would want to vote for them at all.

When all the hubbub finally starts to die down in the evening, it becomes evident that even Tokyo has room for the usual range of noisy urban animal life: stray cats, people's dogs, and crows—crows in such numbers that you will never forget them. The cats seem to delay their most serious confrontations until the moment your head hits the pillow and you turn off the light. The crows chime in later with their avian conversations, usually just before dawn.

wan wan   woof woof, bowwow

Children often refer to dogs as *Wan-chan.*
- *Shiranai hito ga niwa ni hairu tabi ni, inu ga wan wan to hageshiku hoemashita.*
  Whenever a stranger entered the garden, the dog barked furiously.

kyan kyan   yap, yelp of a dog in pain, yip yap of a small dog

- *Kyan kyan nakinagara, kanojo no koinu wa subayaku nigemashita.*
  Her puppy quickly ran away yelping.

nyā nyā   meow

- *Ofuro ni ochita neko wa kawaisō ni nyā nyā naite imashita.*
  The cat had fallen in the bath and was crying pitifully.

goro goro   purr; laze about; lumpy; roll, rumble*

I think *goro goro* sums up perfectly the throaty purr of pleasure
of a contented cat.

- *Terebi no ue ni nete ita neko wa goro goro nodo o narashite
  imashita.*
  The cat sleeping on the television was purring quietly.

poppo   pigeon's coo

- *Yasukuni Jinja de poppo poppo to naite iru hato ni esa o
  nagete yarimashita.*
  We scattered feed for the cooing pigeons at Yasukuni Shrine.

kā kā   caw caw

There are too many crows in Tokyo. Crows live all over Tokyo, but they fly to the alleys of the Ginza early in the morning to feast on the remains of the previous night's reveling, disposed of in flimsy plastic bags awaiting collection by the blue and white garbage vans. A nature park I visited in Meguro Ward recently was so full of circling crows that I thought I had landed in a Hitchcock movie. I think something should be done about them, but there seems to be a tolerance for all sorts of living things in Japan.

• *Karasu ga kā kā nakinagara, negura no hō e tonde ikimashita.*
  Crying caw caw, the crows flew toward their roosting place.

jii jii   cicada's chirp; the sound of something burning*
miin miin   cicada's chirp

Summer has passed as I write this, and I have to imagine a hot, sunny day, heavy with humidity and ringing with the cries of the cicadas. I am often filled with nostalgia when I hear them, but in combination with the merciless heat of a Japanese summer and the relentless pace of a working day here, their drone can at times be very trying. However, I occasionally find myself chanting along with them as I walk home from the subway station, *miin miin miin miin*, eager to escape the heat and, yes, the din.

• *Ichinichijū semi ga jii jii jii, miin miin miin to naite imasu.*
  All day long the cicadas chirrup in the trees.

rin rin   chirp of the *suzumushi* (bush cricket); ringing sound

The *suzumushi* is sometimes called the "bell-ring" insect, and *rin rin* can also refer to the ringing of a small bell. I first came across these insects on the top floor of a Japanese department store, where they were awaiting purchase and rehousing in small insect cages somewhere in a child's room. They make a pretty, high-pitched sound, bringing a welcome bit of the country to a stuffy urban apartment during the long, hot summer nights.

- *Chiisana kago no naka de nihiki no suzumushi ga rin rin to naite imasu.*
  Two bush crickets are singing in the small cage.

Down on the Farm

In 1970, after we had been studying Japanese for about half a year, we went to stay with a family on their dairy farm in Hokkaido.

One of the first things we set out to learn in Japanese were the sounds that farm animals make. Because we all learn these words as children, I think we keep a special fondness for them, so it can come as a shock to discover that familiar, well-loved animal sounds are imitated so differently in a foreign language.

hin hin   neigh

- *Kyūsha kara hin hin to uma no nakigoe ga shimasu.*
  The neighing of horses is coming from the stable.

bū bū   pig's grunt or snort; human griping about something; toot, blow a horn*

- *Onaka o sukashita buta-tachi ga yakamashiku bū bū hana o narashite imashita.*
  The hungry pigs were snorting noisily.

mē mē   goat's or sheep's bleat

You may be surprised to find that the Japanese have a word for a goat's bleat when the animals themselves are so rarely seen in Japan, but friends tell me that before the economic miracle began, many Japanese households kept goats for their milk.

23

- *Nihon de wa yagi wa hijō ni sukunai node, mē mē to iu nakigoe wa metta ni kikarenai.*
Goats are extremely rare in Japan, so you don't often hear their bleating.

mō mō   moo

- *Bokujō de kusa o tabete ita ushi wa yūgata ni naru to, mō mō nakinagara koya e kaerimashita.*
The cows, who had been eating grass in the pasture, returned to their shed when evening fell.

gā gā   duck's quack, goose's honk

- *Ahiru ga gā gā nakinagara, ike o dete, pan o motte ita kodomo ni chikazukimashita.*
The quacking ducks came out of the pond and headed for the children holding bread.

kokekokkō   cock-a-doodle-doo

- *Ondori ga kokekokkō to naita no o kiite, okiru jikan ni natta to wakatta.*
When I heard the rooster crow, I knew it was time to get up.

piyo piyo   cheep cheep

- *Hiyoko ga piyo piyo to nakinagara, oyadori no ato o tsuite kita.*
The cheeping chicks followed their mother.

In the Countryside

From long ago, wild animals in the thick forests and remote

mountains of Japan provided a ready source of material for the fertile imaginations of the local people. They told tales of bewitching foxes, of deceiving badgers and snakes, and of giant baboons lurking deep in the forests. While the woods were magical for the storytellers, they also provided inspiration for the poets, who delighted in the beautiful song of a nightingale or felt sadness upon hearing the lonely hooting of an owl.

The hiker in Japan today will probably have to look hard to discover anything moving on land other than fellow hikers, but he may be lucky and come across a troupe of those favorite scamps of folk tales, the monkeys. Don't be surprised if the locals aren't as pleased by this as you are. Monkeys raid the orchards, steal crops from the fields, and even sometimes pull tiles off the roofs of the houses.

kon kon   fox's yelp; snow falling for a long time; light knocking or coughing

- *Yama de kitsune ga kon kon nakimashita.*
  The fox cried out in the mountains.

kyakkya   monkey's shriek

- *Michiko wa kyakkya to naku saru-tachi no koe o futatabi kiita toki, isoide mado o shimemashita.*
  Michiko shut the windows quickly when she heard the shrieking of the monkeys again.

kakkō   cuckoo's song

- *Kakkō kakkō to naite ita kakkō ga, totsuzen shizuka ni narimashita.*
  The calling cuckoo suddenly became quiet.

hō hokekyo   nightingale's song

- *Uguisu no hō hokekyo hō hokekyo to iu kirei na nakigoe ga nankai mo hibikimashita.*
  The nightingale's beautiful call sounded repeatedly.

hō, hō hō   owl's hooting

- *Hō hō to iu fukurō no nakigoe ga kurayami ni hibikimashita.*
  The owl hooted in the darkness.

pii hyororo   hawk's cry; sound of a flute

- *Tonbi ga pii hyororo to nakinagara kawa no ue ni tonde kimashita.*
  The hawk let out a cry as it came flying over the river.

koro koro   cricket's chirp; ring of a bell; giggling; rolling; plump*

- *Kōrogi ga shi-gokai koro koro to nakimashita.*
  A cricket chirped four or five times in succession.

chinchirorin   cricket's chirp

- *Aki ni natte, furusato ni kaette matsumushi no chinchirorin to iu oto o kiku no o tanoshimi ni shite imasu.*
  I look forward to returning to my home in the country and hearing the chirp of the crickets when autumn comes.

kero kero   frog's croaking

- *Tanbo de kero kero naite iru kaeru no koe o kiku to, yahari furusato wa ii tokoro da to omoimasu.*
  When I hear the frogs croaking in the paddy fields, I think about what a nice place my hometown is after all.

chū chū   mouse's squeak

- *Nezumi ga naya de hitobanjū chū chū naite iru koe ga kikoemashita.*
  We could hear mice squeaking in the barn all night long.

būn, bun bun   buzz of a bee or horsefly

- *Hachi no mure ga su kara bun bun tobitatta.*
  A buzzing swarm of bees flew out of the beehive.

·2·
WEATHER

Summer, fall, winter, spring—every year the four seasons follow one another right on schedule, almost to the day, in Japan. Granted, there are long, rainy intervals in between, when nature has to change the scenery for the next act in her drama. In spite of the predictability, or even perhaps because of it, when people meet they usually greet each other with a reference to the weather. Since it is very unlikely that disagreement will arise over whether it's fine or rainy, hot or cold, the speakers can safely establish a harmonious rapport before moving on to any thorny issues they want to discuss.

Weather assaults our senses and can deeply affect our feelings. It comes as no surprise then that there are many onomatopoeic phrases to describe how we perceive it. When someone mentions the weather, I always try to respond with a slightly unusual comment to delight and, well, impress them. Try to tuck a few of them in your memory to pull out when the chance arises. By the way, I couldn't resist including many phrases having to do with dampness. If you've lived in Japan for a while, you'll know why.

Rain and Dampness

When we lived in a Japanese-style house with no central heating or air conditioning, it could become so damp after a rainy stretch that we used to worry about finding mushrooms growing in our shoes. We still worry, even in our Western-style apartment, but it doesn't happen much anymore.

gusho gusho   soaking wet, sopping wet

- *Niwaka ame ni atte, kasa ga nakatta node, kaisha ni gusho gusho ni nurete tsukimashita.*
  Because I was caught in a sudden rainfall without an umbrella, I arrived at the office sopping wet.

gusshori   drenched

- *Totsuzen no ōame ni atte, karada zentai ga gusshori nurete shimaimashita.*
  I got soaked to the skin in the sudden downpour.

zā zā   sound of a downpour, sound of a lot of water flowing (e.g., a waterfall)

When we first learned this phrase, our Japanese teacher, with great delight, translated it as "raining cats and dogs." If you've ever been in Japan during the rainy season, you'll understand why we never forgot this expression.

- *Hanami ni iku yakusoku o shita hi wa, ainiku asa kara ban made ame ga zā zā furimashita.*
  Unfortunately, on the day we had agreed to go cherry blossom viewing, it rained cats and dogs from morning to evening.

zātto, zatto   sound of a sudden downpour; roughly, approximately

- *Doa o aketa totan, ame ga zātto furihajimemashita.*
  As soon as I opened the door, there was a sudden downpour.

shittori   moist; pleasantly calm and elegant, placid, tranquil*

- *Ame no ato shibafu ga shittori to nurete imashita.*
  The lawn was moist after the rain.

jittori   moist with sweat

- *Reibō ga tsuite ita heya kara deru to, mamonaku karadajū ga jittori asebande kimashita.*
  After I left the air-conditioned room, I soon became damp with sweat from head to toe.

shippori   (affectionate lovers get) thoroughly soaked (in the rain)

- *Wakai futarizure wa harusame ni shippori nuremashita.*
  The young couple got drenched in the spring rain.

shito shito   drizzle; feel damp

- *Ichinichijū ame ga shito shito to futte ita node, kekkyoku zenzen dekakemasen deshita.*
  All day long it drizzled and I didn't go out at all.

jito jito   clammy, feel sticky with dampness

- *Tsuyu no aida wa futon o yoku kawakasenai node, jito jito shita futon ni haitta toki wa kimochi ga warukatta.*
  During the rainy season I couldn't hang the futons out to dry properly, and it was unpleasant because they felt damp.

jime jime   damp; dark, gloomy; depressed, melancholy*

In the heart of the rainy season, no other word seems to describe the atmosphere as well, especially since *jime jime* can also mean gloomy and dark.

- *Maitoshi rokugatsu ni hairu to Nihon no jime jime shita kisetsu ga hajimaru node, watashi wa nigetaku narimasu.*
  Every year when June comes around I know Japan's rainy season is about to begin, and I start wanting to escape.

shobo shobo   drizzle; gloomy; bleary-eyed; depressed*

- *Shobo shobo furu ame ni watashi no sukāto wa sukkari nurete, darashinaku mieta node, sugu uchi e kaerimashita.*
  My skirt got drenched in the depressing drizzle and I looked a slovenly mess, so I went straight home.

dosha dosha   sound of heavily falling rain

The word *dosha* is written with the kanji for earth and sand, and *dosha kuzure* is a landslide, a frequent occurrence in Japan after heavy rains.

- *Mado o aketara dosha dosha to ame ga futte ita.*

  When I opened the window, the rain was pouring down in torrents.

doppuri   steeped or deeply immersed in something (e.g., a bath or soy sauce); in too deep* (used with *tsukaru* or *tsukeru)*
toppuri   pleasantly steeped in (used with *tsukeru* or *tsukaru*); night deepens*

- *Taifū ni yoru ōame de kokumotsu wa doromizu ni doppuri tsukatte shimatta.*

  After the heavy rain of the typhoon, the crops were completely covered with muddy water.

- *Su ni toppuri tsukatta tsukemono o gohan to issho ni tabeta.*

  He ate the pickles steeped in vinegar with his rice.

bara bara   (rain or hail) pelts down; be thinly scattered or disorganized

- *Mayonaka ni totsuzen hyō ga bara bara to furihajimeta node, patto me ga samemashita.*

  I woke up suddenly when hail began to pelt down in the middle of the night.

- *Kodomo ga asobi ni kite ita node, heya no naka wa omocha ga bara bara ni chirakatte imashita.*

  After the children came to play, the room was littered with toys.

bisha bisha   dripping wet; splashing
bisho bisho   sound of fairly heavy rainfall; get soaked
bisshori   very wet, soaked

- *Nagagutsu o haita kodomo wa, mizutamari o bisha bisha to aruki, doromizu o hanetobashimashita.*
  The children in boots splashed about in the muddy puddles.
- *Ame ga bisho bisho futta node, watashi no haregi wa bisshori nurete shimaimashita.*
  My best clothes got soaking wet in the pouring rain.

bicha bicha   sound of a small amount of water splashing; thoroughly soaked or flooded

- *Kodomo ga warainagara mizutamari no aida o bicha bicha to hashirimawatte imashita.*
  The children ran laughing through the puddles of water.

moya moya   foggy, hazy, misty; blurred; unclear, uncertain; gloomy
moyatto   misty, foggy; dazed

- *Kyanpujō de asa okitara kiri ga moyatto to mizuumi o ōtte imashita.*
  When we woke up in the morning at the campsite, mist blanketed the lake.

Cold and Snow

Whew! It's good to be out of the rain. The cold, clear days of late fall and winter come as a huge relief after the hot, humid summer and early autumn drizzle. It usually snows once or twice a year in Tokyo, and much more often in the mountains and on the Japan Sea side. Whether it's of taking a hot bath, drinking warm saké, gently thawing cold toes with a traditional Japanese foot warmer, or *kotatsu,* or staying at a snow-covered thatched farmhouse with its welcoming open hearth, some of our nicest memories of Japan will always be of keeping warm in winter.

zawa zawa   chilly; rustling sound; clamor of a crowd

- *Nan to naku zawa zawa shita kanji ga suru. Dō yara kaze o hiita rashii.*
  I feel chilly. I think I've caught a cold.
- *Kogarashi de ura no takeyabu ga zawa zawa to shite imasu.*
  The bamboo behind my house rustle noisily in the cold, wintry wind.

sū sū   a draft; sound of nasal breathing

- *Ie no naka ni sū sū to sukimakaze ga hairikonde kimashita.*
  A cold draft snuck into the house.

zoku zoku   shiver due to the cold; shiver with excitement or pleasure; shiver in fear; things happen one after another

Japanese have traditionally associated fear with feeling cold, so much so that horror films used to be shown in the summer, before the days of air-conditioning, to induce a cold shiver in the audiences as a form of relief from the summer heat. Ghost stories are also told in the summer for this reason.

- *Kibishii samusa no tame karada zentai ga zoku zoku shita.*
  In the fierce cold, a chill crept over my whole body.
- *Nisshabyō de kenbutsunin ga zoku zoku to taoremashita.*
  The spectators collapsed one after another in the heat.

zotto   a cold shiver down one's spine

In this case, the shivering is caused not by cold but by fear.

- *Ano osoroshii jiken o omoidasu to zotto shimasu.*
  Whenever I think of that horrible incident, my blood runs cold.

hiyari   shudder due to cold, feel a sudden chill; momentarily panic-striken

hiyatto   suddenly feel cold or very frightened

hiya hiya   feel cold continuously; shudder; feel nervous or frightened

- *Akiko wa tsumetai mono o kubisuji ni oshitsukerarete hiyatto shimashita.*
  When the cold object was pressed against Akiko's neck, she felt a sudden chill.

- *Doa o nagaku akeppanashi ni shita tame ni hiya hiya shita kūki ga haitte kimashita.*

Because the door was left open a long time, cold air had come into the room.

- *Kodomo ga jikkai no mado kara mi o noridashita node hiya hiya shita.*

  I felt scared to death when the child leaned out of the tenth story window.

hin'yari   cool

- *Hin'yari to shita yoru no kaze ni atatte, kibun ga sukkiri shimashita.*

  The pleasant, cool breeze in the evening refreshed my spirits.

jin, jiin   numbing cold; ringing vibration; feel like you are going to cry; pins and needles*

- *Niigata e sukii ni itta toki, yoru ni naru to samukute jiin to narimashita.*

  When we went skiing in Niigata, it always became numbingly cold after nightfall.

chira chira   fluttering of snow or falling blossoms; occasional glimpses; flickering light; twinkling of stars*

- *Yoru ni yuki ga chira chira furidashimashita.*

  At night, snow began to flutter down quietly.

shin shin   snow falls thick and fast

- *Yuki ga shin shin to furu node, watashi wa moshi gakkō ga sukkari yuki ni uzumorete shimattara dō shitara ii darō ka to kangaedashimashita.*

  As the snow fell thick and fast, I started to think of what I should do if the school were snowed in.

Heat

It isn't that it gets all that hot in Japan in summer, it's just that the heat is constant. It doesn't cool down very much in the evening, or even after a rain shower. Pretty circular fans, wind bells, and chilled bottles of beer help to ease the discomfort, but no one looks forward to summer much. It's the spring and autumn that delight the Japanese.

kakka continuous heat or light; blush; hot sensation; burn with rage*

- *Kakka to teritsukeru natsu no taiyō no tame ni, niwa ni ueta pechuniya ga karete shimatta.*
  The petunias I planted in the garden withered in the scorching heat of the summer sun.

kan kan blazing heat or sun; clang, high clear ring*; very angry*

- *Natsu no tokai no kan kan deri ga gaman dekinaku natte, yama no suzushii hishochi ni nigemashita.*
  I couldn't bear the torrid summer heat in the city, so I escaped to a cool resort in the mountains.

gira gira intense glaring sunlight; dazzling light (like *kira kira* but stronger)

- *Gira gira to teritsukeru taiyō no moto de karada o yakinagara, hiyakedome kuriimu o zenbu tsukatte shimaimashita.*
  While sunbathing in the blazing sunshine, I used up all my sunscreen.

bota bota continuous dripping
pota pota continuous dripping (lighter sound than *bota bota)*, plop plop

- *Natsu ni wa maiasa hitai kara pota pota ase o nagashinagara kaisha ni ikimashita.*
  Every morning in summer I went to the office with sweat dripping from my forehead.

mutto   stifling; sulky, look angry*

- *Natsu ni reibō ga nakatta koro wa jimusho wa atsukute, mutto shita.*
  Before air-conditioning, offices were hot and stifling in summer.

mun mun   humid; sultry*

- *Mun mun suru hi ga tsuzuita node, sukkari tsukarete shimaimashita.*
  The hot sultry days continued one after another, and I became completely exhausted.

- *Kyō wa densha no naka ga mun mun shite ita node sukkari tsukarete shimaimashita.*
  I was completely exhausted today because of the stuffy air in the train.

yura yura   (image) wavers (in the hot air)

- *Saboten ga sabaku no nekki de yura yura shite mieru.*
  The cacti seem to be wavering in the hot desert air.

Dryness

It can get rather dry in winter in Japan, but no one worries about it much, unless she has very dry skin or a valuable old lacquer collection. Dry is generally synonymous with good weather in Japanese.

kara kara   very dry; empty; laugh with a high-pitched voice; clatter*; parched*

- *Kono fuyu wa kara kara no tenki ga tsuzuite iru node Tōkyō de wa kaji ga ōi darō.*
  Because we are having very dry weather this winter, there will probably be many fires in Tokyo.

karatto   weather clears up; crisp*

- *Ame ga totsuzen yande, karatto hareagatta.*
  The rain suddenly stopped and it cleared up.

karari   dry, clear; clatter; cheerful*; crisp*

- *Karari to hareta aki no hibi o Tōhoku de tanoshiku sugoshita.*
  I passed the dry, clear days of autumn enjoyably in Tohoku.

sarari   fresh and dry; smooth action, slide; carefree, easygoing*

- *Shūmatsu wa sarari to shita sawayaka na tenki de, yama nobori ni saikō datta.*
  The weather on the weekend was fresh and bright; perfect for mountain climbing.

Cloudiness, Wind, and Storms

The great eastern storm is, of course, the typhoon. Some years go by without any typhoons, while other years seem to have them one after the other. My most memorable typhoon occurred on a summer night about ten years ago when we had just moved into an early Showa period Western-style house. The rain and wind started about midnight. We could not figure out how to shut the old-fashioned windows properly, and we spent several frantic hours running from room to room, mopping up pools of water that were collecting on the floors.

The weather after a storm can, however, be very pleasant, with gentle breezes blowing and fluffy clouds overhead.

don'yori   overcast, gloomy, dull

- *Hayaoki suru tsumori datta keredomo, don'yori to shita sora o mite, mata nete shimaimashita.*
  I intended to get up early, but when I saw the overcast sky I went back to sleep.

pokkari   float up; suddenly appear; open wide

- *Kōen ni pikunikku ni itta toki, aozora ni wa pokkari kumo ga ukande imashita.*
  Clouds were floating in the blue sky when we went to the park for a picnic.

fuwa fuwa   light, buoyant, fluffy, soft; giddy; frivolous*

- *Yama no ue ni kumo ga fuwa fuwa to ukande imashita.*
  Fluffy clouds were floating over the mountains.

funwari   gently floating; soft or puffy appearance

- *Haru no atatakai hi sanpo ni dekakete, funwari ukande iru kumo o nagamete tanoshimimashita.*
  I enjoyed watching the gently floating clouds as I went for a walk on a warm spring day.

moku moku   billow up; do something in silence*

- *Natsu ni naru to nyūdōgumo ga moku moku to arawareru no ga miraremasu.*
  In summer, cumulonimbus clouds can be seen billowing up in the sky.

soyo soyo   light breeze

- *Soyo soyo to fuku harukaze no naka de hata ga hatameite ita.*
  The flags fluttered in the gentle spring breeze.

hyū hyū   whistle; asthmatic wheeze
byū byū   whistle (stronger than *hyū hyū*)
pyū pyū   shrill whistle

- *Kogarashi ga pyū pyū to fukihajimeru to toshinose wa mō me no mae desu.*
  Once the winter wind begins to whistle, it can't be long until the year's end.

goro goro   rumble, roll; lumpy; laze about; purr*

- *Sora ga kuraku natte goro goro to enrai no nibui oto ga kikoete kimashita.*
  After the sky became dark, you could hear the rumble of the distant thunder.

pikatto   flash of lightning

- *Arashi no mattadanaka sora ga inazuma de pikatto hikatte taihen kowakatta.*
  It was very frightening when the sky lit up with the flash of lightning during the storm.

Nighttime

toppuri   night deepens; pleasantly steeped in*

- *Kaisha no pikunikku kara ie ni kaetta koro ni wa hi wa toppuri kurete imashita.*
  By the time we returned home from the company picnic it was already nightfall.

kira kira   twinkle, glitter, shine

- *Tanbo o ōu yozora wa kira kira to kagayaku hoshi de ippai deshita.*
  The night sky over the paddy fields was full of brightly twinkling stars.

pika pika   stars shine brightly; brand new

- *Akachōchin de nonda kaerimichi, pika pika hikaru hoshi wa Kinsei mitai deshita.*
  When I came back from my drinking place, I saw a brilliant star I thought was Venus.

chika chika   flicker (of stars), flash (of lights); irritated (eyes)
chira chira   twinkling of stars; flickering light; occasional glimpses;
fluttering of snow or falling blossoms*

* *Chira chira matataku hoshi o nagai koto nagamete imashita.*
  I gazed at the twinkling stars for a long, long time.

shin, shiin   utterly quiet
* *Yuki ga furu to atari wa shin to shizumarikaerimasu.*
  When it snows, the world around us becomes utterly silent.

· 3 ·
FOOD

Foreigners have always had ambivalent feelings about Japanese food. Dried seaweed, raw fish, vegetables cut in fantastic shapes, bitter green tea—it's so unlike what we're accustomed to at home. I think the Japanese want us to like their food, all the more because they suspect we don't. Some of their eating habits seem barbaric and macabre to us, whether it's eating *sashimi* cut from live fish right before their eyes, serving loaches that burrow into tofu to avoid being boiled alive, or drinking glasses of turtle blood to increase their stamina. Even if you have to come to terms with how you feel about the food, it helps to break the ice if you can honestly say you like one or two of the known "throat stoppers," like *nattō* (sticky, fermented soybeans) or *takuan* (a type of pickled radish that is bright yellow).

Preparation and Cooking

I was watching daytime television one day when, to my surprise, a blond foreigner appeared and proceeded to present a cooking program in Japanese. She spiced her cooking instructions with English-language proverbs and adages, giving a little English lesson on the side. I found the program very entertaining in spite of my lack of interest in learning to prepare what she was fixing. With the intense interest of the Japanese in everyone's eating habits, food preparation comes up as a topic of conversation more often than you might expect, and you may find yourself unexpectedly having to explain how you whipped up that delightful little Caesar salad or cheese soufflé. It is also very likely that sometime someone will regale you with detailed instructions on how to prepare a special delicacy of Japanese cuisine that you have admired when dining with him.

gutsu gutsu   simmer, boil

- *Sukiyaki ga gutsu gutsu to niete kite umasō da.*
  The sukiyaki came to a delicious-sounding simmer.

karari   crisp; clatter; dry, clear*; cheerful*

- *Abura de jagaimo o karari to agete kudasai.*
  Fry the potatoes in oil until crispy.

kura kura   boil; feel dizzy
gura gura   boil; fickle; tremor; rickety; loose*

- *Yakan no o-yu ga gura gura waite ita.*
  The water in the kettle was boiling.

koto koto   simmer, boil lightly, rattle
goto goto   boil vigorously, heavy rattle

- *Mame o yowabi de koto koto to ichijikan gurai nikonda.*
  She boiled the beans on a low flame for about an hour.

saku saku   cut (a crisp vegetable); crunch (while eating or walking on snow)

- *Kanojo wa hōchō de tamanegi o saku saku to kitta.*
  She chopped the onion crisply with a kitchen knife.

jii jii   sound of something burning; cicada's chirp*

- *Chotto me o hanashita suki ni sutēki no abura ga jii jii to kogetsukimashita.*
  When I wasn't keeping an eye on it, the fat on the steak began burning.

47

jā jā   sizzle (in oil); pour, hose down

- *Tamanegi o furaipan de jā jā to itamete imasu.*
  The sizzling onions are frying in the pan.

jabu jabu   stir strongly; splash about

The popular dish *shabu shabu* (boiled meat with a dipping sauce) takes its name from an onomatopoeia that described a light stirring movement.

- *Kare wa tomato sūpu ni gyūniku to tamanegi nado o jabu jabu irete sono hi no yūhan ni shita.*
  He made his supper by putting beef and onions in tomato soup, and stirring it briskly.

jū jū   hiss, sizzle

- *Guriru ni noseta sōsēji ga jū jū yakete kita.*
  The sausages were sizzling on the grill.

jiri jiri   sizzle; ring; fierce sunlight; little by little, gradually

- *Niku no aburami ga jiri jiri to kogetsuite kimashita.*
  The meat's fat sizzled as it became scorched.

shinnari   soft, flexible

- *Tamanegi o shinnari suru made itamete kara, omuretsu ni iremasu.*
  After frying the onions until they are soft, add them to the omelette.

tara tara   running, dripping; complain endlessly*
dara dara   heavy dripping, running; tedious; slovenly; gentle slope

- *Naomi-chan wa hachimitsu o tara tara nagareru hodo pan ni nuritsuketa.*
  Naomi poured honey all over the bread until it was overflowing.

para para   dry and loose; light sprinkling (of rain); flip through

- *Potāju ni paseri to parumezan chiizu o para para to furikaketa.*
  She sprinkled parsley and Parmesan cheese on the *potage*.

hita hita   thin covering of water; lapping water (on the side of a boat); approach gradually

- *Kawa o muita jagaimo o hita hita no mizu ni irete okimashita.*
  I left the peeled potatoes covered with water.

buku buku   sound of bubbling; swish fluid in one's mouth; swollen and fat*

- *Gohan ga buku buku awadatte kitara hi o yowameru.*
  Once the rice begins to boil, lower the heat.

butsu butsu   chop; simmer; having many small holes; have a rash; mutter, grumble*

- *Piiman o butsu butsu ni kitte, sarada no ue ni nosete kara doresshingu o kakemasu.*
  After chopping the green peppers and placing them on top of the salad, add dressing.

Hunger and Eating

Stomachs rumble when we're hungry and in Japan it's not considered rude to make a lot of noise when we eat. Words describing the sounds of eating and of stomachs grumbling are quite numerous in Japanese.

gatsu gatsu   greedy, hungry

- *Yōyaku tabemono ga dasarete, minna gatsu gatsu tabemashita.*
  When the food was finally served, everyone ate greedily.

gū gū   stomach rumbles; gurgle; snoring sound*

- *Asagohan o taberu jikan ga nakatta node, jūichiji goro kara hara ga gū gū naridashita.*
  I didn't have time to eat breakfast, so from about eleven o'clock my stomach started rumbling.

kucha kucha   chewing sound; crumple

- *Kucha kucha oto o tatete mono o taberu nante gyōgi ga warui yo.*
  It's bad manners to make that chomping noise when you eat.

suru suru   slurp; move smoothly
zuru zuru   slurp; sound of a heavy object being dragged; lose repeatedly; slowly slip backward*
tsuru tsuru   slurp vigorously; slippery; smooth; bald

- *Kare wa udon o tsuru tsuru to oishisō ni tabemashita.*
  He slurped down the noodles with gusto.
- *Satoimo wa tsuru tsuru shite ite, hashi de tabenikui.*
  Taro is slippery and hard to eat with chopsticks.

tappuri   full, oodles, plenty

The phrase "volume tappuri" (a large helping) was very common when we first came to Japan. Noting that foreigners generally ate more than they did, our Japanese hosts seemed concerned about whether we had enough to eat when we were with them.

- *Kono nabemono ryōri ni wa yasai ga tappuri haitte iru yo.*
  There are lots of vegetables in this stew.

torotto   melt in your mouth; glutinous, syrupy; dull eyes*; sleep lightly for a short period*

- *Sono batā ame o kuchi ni ireru to, torotto tokete amai yo.*
  When you put that butter candy in your mouth, it melts and tastes sweet.

paku paku   vigorous eating, gobble; flap open

- *Shigoto ga owatte kara, yūshoku o paku paku tabeta.*
  After finishing work, they wolfed down their supper.

bari bari   munch; tear, scratch; work energetically*
pari pari   chew vigorously; stiff (collar); brand-new; eager; devoted*

- *Eiga o minagara, Ken to Mari wa bari bari to senbei o tabete ita.*
  While watching the movie, Ken and Mari were munching rice crackers.
- *Tsukemono o kuchi ni irete, ha de pari pari to oto o tateta.*
  He put the pickles in his mouth and crunched them noisily.

peko peko   ravenously hungry; kowtow*

- *Okāsan! Onaka peko peko yo!*
  Mom! I'm starving!

perori eat up (not as brief as *perotto*); lick quickly; stick out one's tongue

perotto swallow in one mouthful, eat a lot in a very short time

- *Kare wa taihen na ōgui de, udon sanbai perotto tabete shimatta.*
  He is such a glutton; he finished three bowls of noodles in one sitting.

bero bero lick vigorously (more heavily than *pero pero*); dead drunk*

pero pero lick, poke tongue out repeatedly

- *Kodomo wa pero pero to roripoppu o namete imasu.*
  The child is licking a lollypop.

bori bori crunch, munch; scratch

pori pori crunch, munch; scratch (lighter sound than *bori bori*)

- *Akira wa senbei o bori bori to kajitte ita.*
  Akira was munching rice crackers loudly.

musha musha munch (on a softer food than *pori pori*); eat greedily, devour

- *Gakkō no kaerimichi, kodomo ga hoshiika o musha musha tabete ita.*
  The children were munching dried squid on their way home from school.

mogu mogu chew softly; mumble

- *Kōsuke wa niku no katamari o kuchi ni irete, shibaraku mogu mogu to kuchi o ugokashite ita.*
  Kosuke put the piece of meat in his mouth and chewed on it for some time.

moso moso munch (something dry); mumble; wriggle, fidget

- *Ushi ga moso moso to hoshikusa o tabete ita.*
  The cow was munching his hay.

mori mori eat hard; work hard; full of zest or ambition*

- *Kare wa mori mori tabete mori mori hataraku hito da.*
  He's a fellow who eats hard and works hard.

Taste

Many of these phrases describe how a food feels in the mouth rather than the actual taste.

assari light, delicate (flavor); openhearted, easygoing*

This is the perfect word to use when you want to say something nice about a food that has almost no taste.

- *Aā, assari shita aji desu ne.*
  Ah, it has a delicate flavor, doesn't it?

kasu kasu   dry; just barely reach a standard level (lifestyle) or deadline

- *Kono ringo wa kasu kasu de aji ga nai.*
  This apple is dry and tasteless.

karatto   crisp; weather clears up*

- *Karatto ageta tenpura wa oishikatta.*
  The crispy tenpura was a real treat.

kari kari   crisp, crunchy; worked up*

- *Bangohan ni kari kari ni ageta furaido chikin to sarada o tabeta.*
  I had a salad and crispy fried chicken for supper.
- *Boku no tomodachi no daikōbutsu wa kari kari no umezuke da.*
  My friend loves crunchy pickled plums.

gari gari   rock hard; scratching; thin; obsessed

- *Kono jagaimo wa mada gari gari da.*
  These potatoes are still rock hard.

gusha gusha   squashed and runny, splat, crumple; messy; ruin

- *Akiko-chan ga kago ni haitta tamago o otoshite minna gusha gusha ni shite shimatta.*
  Akiko dropped the carton of eggs and they were all broken and runny.

gucha gucha   mushy and wet; chew, suck; messy; complain*

- *Banana wa gucha gucha ni natte shimatte taberarenakatta.*
  The banana had become mushy, so I couldn't eat it.

kochi kochi   rock hard; tense; stubborn, inflexible*
gochi gochi   rock hard (harder than *kochi kochi*)

• *Tsukitate no mochi mo tsugi no hi ni wa kochi kochi ni naru.*
  Freshly made rice cakes get hard by the next day.

kote kote   smother; rich food; paint (makeup) on thick
kotteri   rich, heavy food; smothered in; paint (makeup) on thick

• *Batā o kote kote ni nutta pan o itsumo tabete iru to futorimasu yo.*
  You'll get fat if you're always eating bread smothered in butter.
• *Fuyu no samui hi ni, kotteri shita aji no shichū o taberu no wa saikō da.*
  On a cold winter's day, eating a full-bodied stew is wonderful.

kori kori   rubbery; stiff (shoulders); firm muscle*
gori gori   hard, rough; crunch (chewing on a hard object like a bone); scratch

• *Shinsen na awabi wa kori kori shite ite oishii.*
  Fresh abalone has a firm texture and is delicious.
• *Sono nashi wa mada gori gori shite ite taberarenai.*
  That pear is still hard so I can't eat it.

kongari   nicely browned, tan

• *Kongari to yaketa o-mochi o taberu to o-shōgatsu o omoidasu.*
  Whenever I eat toasted rice cakes I think of New Year's.

sappari   refreshing; not at all; open, fresh and simple*

• *Yōguruto no sappari shita aji wa saikin taihen ninki ga aru.*

The refreshing flavor of yogurt has become very popular recently.

shiko shiko   pleasantly firm texture (in mouth)

- *Shiko shiko shite iru soba wa ichiban oishii desu.*
  Firm noodles taste the best.

shaki shaki   crisp (fruit or vegetables); brisk*

- *Kodomo wa shaki shaki shita hazawari no ringo ga daisuki da.*
  My child loves snacks like crisp apples.

shakitto   fresh and crisp (in mouth or to touch); a fresh feeling

- *Saba o su de shimeru to shakitto shite oishii.*
  When you put mackerel in vinegar, it becomes firm and delicious.

shari shari   crisp, tangy, fresh; scrape

- *Shābetto wa aisu kuriimu to chigatte shari shari shite iru.*
  Unlike ice cream, sherbet has a fresh, tangy taste.
- *Kakigōri wa natsu matsuri no meibutsu de, supūn de shari shari kakimazenagara taberu.*
  Shaved ice is a specialty of summer festivals that you scrape and mix with a spoon to eat.

sukatto   fresh, clean; clear

- *Kōra wa sukatto sawayaka na nomimono desu.*
  Cola is a drink with a clean and refreshing taste.

tsun, tsūn   stinging, pungent (e.g., ammonia or vinegar); pointed; standoffish*

This phrase describes a stinging sensation in the nose, as felt when you eat something like horseradish.

- *Wasabi o kuchi ni ireta toki, hana ni tsūn to kita.*
  When I put the Japanese horseradish in my mouth, my sinuses cleared.

dorotto   thick, sticky liquid

- *Samui hi ni dorotto shita potāju wa saikō desu.*
  On a cold day, a thick *potage* is the best.

toro toro   melted; weak fire; doze off

- *Yaita mashumaro no hyōmen wa karitto shite, naka wa toro toro ni tokete iru.*
  The toasted marshmallow's outside was crispy, and the inside was nicely melted.

doro doro   muddy, jelly-like; rumble; troublesome

- *Doro doro ni natta nimono wa mazukatta.*
  The food had been boiled to a pulp and tasted terrible.

nechi nechi   stick firmly; tenacious (in a bad way), be a pest*

- *Sono kyarameru wa ha ni nechi nechi kuttsuite tabezurai desu.*
  That caramel is hard to eat because it firmly sticks to your teeth.

neto neto   unpleasantly sticky and wet

- *Reizōko no oku ni irete oita nokorimono wa neto neto ni natte shimatta.*
  The leftovers in the back of the refrigerator eventually became wet and sticky.

neba neba sticky (not necessarily unpleasant)

- *Nihonjin wa neba neba shita nattō ga suki da.*
  Japanese like sticky fermented soybeans.

basa basa dry and crumbling, stale; rustle; messy (hairstyle); flap
pasa pasa dry, stale; flutter

- *Kono pan wa pasa pasa shite umakunai.*
  This bread is dry, stale, and tasteless.
- *Yoku gaimai wa pasa pasa shite iru to iwaremasu.*
  It is often said that foreign rice tastes dry.

paritto crisp; fresh and new

- *Nori no oishisa wa paritto shita hazawari da.*
  The delicious taste of dried seaweed comes from its crisp, fresh feel when you bite it.

hiri hiri piquant
piri piri spicy food (more spicy than *hiri hiri*); blow a whistle; rip; nervous; prickling pain*

- *Kono Chūka ryōri wa hiri hiri suru.*
  This Chinese food is piquant.
- *Kono karē wa Indo no kōshinryō ga piri piri kiite ite ikeru.*
  The Indian spices in this curry are hot, making it really delicious.

puri puri firm flesh; be in a huff*

- *Puri puri shita iki no ii sakana o katte kita.*
  I bought nice, firm, fresh fish.

beta beta sticky, pasted; a couple falling all over each other*

- *Ano mochi wa beta beta to ha ni kuttsuku.*
  Those rice cakes stick to the teeth.

hoka hoka   nicely steaming, hot food; feel warm and pleasant

- *Manjū ga hoka hoka to yuge o tatete oishisō da.*
  The steaming dumplings look delicious.

hoku hoku   soft and tasty (baked, starchy food); pleased, beaming

- *Hoku hoku ni yakiagatta o-imo wa oishisō da.*
  The freshly baked potato looks delicious.

bosotto   stale; mumble; unsociable
boso boso   stale; mumble

- *Boso boso shita pan o kōra de nagashikonda.*
  I washed down the dry, stale bread with a cola.

hoya hoya   food hot from the oven; fresh state (for both people and things)*

- *Kono gyūnyū wa shiboritate no hoya hoya desu.*
  This milk is fresh from the cow.

horotto   nice bitter taste; slight stimulation of the senses; feel pleasure or sympathy; something light and small falling (e.g., a tear); tipsy*

- *Ano biiru wa horotto shita nigami ga aru.*
  That beer has a bitter taste.

poro poro   dry and crumbly; (tears) fall one after another

- *Oishii gohan to wa poro poro shite inakute, yawarakaku tsuya ga aru mono da.*
  To be really tasty, rice must not be crumbly or dry, and it should be soft and have a sheen.

· 4 ·
WORK

When I started to learn Japanese in 1969, there was almost no one studying the language in order to improve their business performance or even to earn a living here. Most of us plugged away for the sheer sake of scholarship or improved social communication. Today, both in Japan and overseas, many work opportunities for Westerners require at least a knowledge of spoken Japanese. And these days there are so many of us wanting to work and live in Japan that we must do everything we can to improve our competitiveness in the job market, or risk finding that the only source of income available is teaching English conversation. I hear that even that formerly fertile field of employment is now nearly saturated with instructors.

For a time in the eighties, my workplace was in the office of a foreign bank in Tokyo. I wasn't working for the bank, but I made a lot of friends there and often listened to their concerns about making a profit in Japan. In the seventies, I worked in a big Japanese company where the bilingual Japanese president of the firm was very fond of the phrase "to sell like hot cakes." Until I undertook my research for this book, I didn't realize that there were a number of equivalent Japanese phrases translated in Japanese-English dictionaries as "to sell like hot cakes."

For all of you trying to make a living in or outside Japan, or hoping to do so in the future, here are some useful workplace-related onomatopoeic phrases. And should you ever find yourself trying to market a product in Japan, may you enjoy the good fortune of having it sell like hot cakes.

Feelings, Attitudes, and Approaches to Work

Although some of these phrases don't apply exclusively to working, all of them relate to how a person feels when working and how he or she approaches the situations that arise in the workplace.

atafuta   flustered, in a hurry

- *Hōkokusho no machigai ni ki ga tsuita toki, atafuta to kachō o sagashi ni ikimashita.*
  When he noticed the mistake in the report, he rushed off to find his section chief.

dogimagi   flustered, lose composure

- *Mondai ga okiru tabi ni kanojo wa dogimagi shimasu.*
  Whenever there's a problem, she gets flustered.
- *Dareka ni Eigo de hanashikakerareru to dogimagi shite zenzen henji ga dekinai.*
  When someone addresses me in English, I lose my composure and can't reply at all.

unzari   fed up, sick and tired

- *Keiji wa mainichi no zangyō ni unzari shite shimatta.*
  Keiji finally got sick and tired of working overtime every day.
- *Natsu no mushiatsui tenki ni unzari shita.*
  I got fed up with the hot, humid summer weather.

etchira otchira   toil, laboring; things not going smoothly

- *Jimusho no omotai chōdohin o etchira otchira ugokashita.*
  Struggling, we moved the heavy office furniture.

kichi kichi   do something just so; tight schedule
kitchiri   tight schedule; exact; well-fitting; tight (cork)

I know from personal experience that schedules in Japan are never anything but tight.

- *Gozenchū dake de mittsu mo kaigi ga aru nante, totemo kichi kichi kunde aru sukejūru da.*
  With three meetings all in the morning, it's really a tight schedule.
- *Suzuki wa banji ni kichi kichi shisugite iru node, angai shōshin shinai darō.*
  Suzuki does everything too meticulously so contrary to expectation, I don't think he'll be promoted quickly.

kiri kiri   so busy you seem to be spinning; sharp continuous pain*

- *Getsumatsu wa kaikei no keisan no tame ni shigoto de kiri kiri mai shite ita.*
  At the end of the month, I was up to my neck in work doing the calculations for the accounts.

kotsu kotsu   work at over a long period; sound of hard shoes clicking on the pavement; knocking or rapping sound

- *Kotsu kotsu to kenkyū o tsuzukete, yōyaku subarashii kekka o tassei shita.*
  He worked hard at his research and in the end achieved excellent results.

kossori   do something in secret

- *Kare wa kossori to kakureru yō ni konpyūtā gēmu o yatte imashita.*
  He was secretly playing a computer game.

shaki shaki   brisk; crisp (fruit or vegetables)*

- *Ano shinnyū shain wa shaki shaki to shite ite, hontō ni ii inshō o ataemasu.*

That new employee is a go-getter and really makes a good impression.

zuba zuba   straight-talking; directly

* *Shachō ni zuba zuba iken ga ieru node hira shain no naka de kare dake ga yakuinkai ni yobareta.*
Because he dares to tell it like it is to the president, he was the only ordinary employee invited to the directors' meeting.

seka seka   busily, unsettled, rushing, busybody

* *Amerika honsha no shain ga tsugi tsugi to rainichi shita node, Hiroko wa seka seka to hataraita.*
Because visitors from the head office in America kept coming to Japan, Hiroko worked like mad.

sesse   busily, work hard

- *Shain wa sesse to nenji sōkai no junbi o shite ita.*
  The employees were busy as bees preparing for the annual general meeting.

taji taji   cannot hold one's own; be thrown off balance*

- *Kare no tsuyoi settoku ryoku ni watakushi wa taji taji ni natte, hakkiri shita henji ga dekinakatta.*
  Confronted with his strong powers of persuasion, I was at a loss for words and could not respond clearly.

chiguhagu   disorganized, haywire; not match, out of harmony*

- *Atarashii jimusho ni utsutte kara, nanimo kamo chiguhagu de, shibaraku shigoto ga umaku ikanakatta.*
  For a while after moving to the new office, everything was disorganized and work didn't go well.

chakkari   shrewd, cunning; having sound business sense

- *Ken wa Jun to chigatte, genjitsuteki de chakkari shite imasu.*
  Unlike Jun, Ken is realistic and shrewd.

chiyahoya   butter someone up, curry favor

- *Kare wa taezu mawari kara chiyahoya sarete iru node, wagamama ni natta.*
  Because he is constantly buttered up by those around him, he has become self-centered.

chanto   do properly, correctly, exactly; perfectly

- *Yamamoto-san wa itsumo chanto shigoto o shite imasu.*

Yamamoto always does his work properly.
- *Chanto yōfuku o kinasai.*
  You must dress properly.

tsuke tsuke   blunt, speak one's mind without hesitation
zuke zuke   blunt, speak one's mind without hesitation (in a more direct way than *tsuke tsuke*)

- *Aitsu wa itsumo zuke zuke hihan suru node, boku wa chigau bu ni utsuritai.*
  I want to move to a different department because he always criticizes me mercilessly.

norari kurari   vague, beat around the bush; laze around*

- *Kyūka o seikyū suru toki, kachō wa itsumo norari kurari to hakkiri shita henji o kurenai.*
  Whenever I ask for time off, my section chief always beats around the bush and won't give me a clear answer.

bassari   decide resolutely; sever completely

- *Boku ga nagai jikan o kakete chūi bukaku hon'yaku shita repōto wa, henshūsha ni hon kara bassari sakujo sareta.*
  The report I'd spent a long time carefully translating was cut right out of the book by the editor.

bari bari   work energetically; scratch, tear; munch*
pari pari   devoted; stiff (collar); brand-new; eager; chew vigorously*

- *Shain ga bari bari hataraku node shitenchō wa yorokonda.*
  The employees were working hard so the manager was happy.
- *Shigoto o bari bari yaru ōeru ya shufu-tachi ni, rediisu komikku wa hijō ni ninki ga aru.*

Comics targeting women are very popular among hard-working female office workers and housewives.

bura bura　waste time, idle; dangle

- *Yotei yori hayaku owatta node, tsugi no kaigi ga hajimaru made bura bura shite ita.*
  I'd finished ahead of schedule, so I was just killing time until the next conference began.

peko peko　kowtow; ravenously hungry*

- *Dare ni atte mo peko peko shinakya naranai kara, sērusuman wa tsumaranai.*
  A salesman's life is no fun, having to kowtow to everyone you meet.

uka uka　dream away one's time; lack direction or a plan; careless; settled
ukkari　inadvertently, carelessly, thoughtlessly

- *Uka uka shite iru to kongetsu no sērusu no mokuhyōgaku wa tassei dekinai.*
  If you just dream away your time, you won't be able to achieve this month's sales target.

guzu guzu　make slow progress, dillydally; sniffle; complain*

- *Kare no yō na guzu guzu shite iru otoko wa, kichin to shigoto o shiagenai darō.*
  A fellow who dillydallies like that never finishes his work properly.

bosa bosa　idle; absentminded; disheveled
bosatto　idle; absentminded; blank expression

- *Bosa bosa shite iru to, torinokosareru yo.*
  If you're idle, you'll fall behind.

bon'yari   loaf about; absentminded; blurred, indistinct*

- *Ano teinen majika no shain wa mainichi bon'yari shite kaeru jikan o matte iru dake da.*
  That employee who is retiring this year does nothing every day but sit around woolgathering until it's time to go home.

mago mago   hang around; confused

- *Mago mago shite iru to, kyōsō aite no X-sha ga don don keiyaku o musunde shimaimasu yo.*
  While you're hanging around doing nothing, your competitor, Company X is busy getting new contracts.

mecha kucha   incoherent; confused, messy; preposterous; destroyed
mecha mecha   all screwed up, disorderly; logically inconsistent; in a mess

We foreigners always get things out of order in Japan. I constantly seem to need this phrase. *Mecha kucha* means almost the same thing as *mecha mecha* but in a less concrete, more nonsensical way. It could, for example, describe an exorbitant price for an antique in poor condition.

- *Sono hito no ronshi wa mecha mecha da.*
  That person's argument is illogical.
- *Ano rōdō kumiai no chin'age yōkyū wa mecha kucha da.*
  That union's demand for a wage hike is preposterous.
- *Ano shimidarake no obi ga ichiman en da to wa mecha kucha na nedan da!*
  That dirty old obi is going for ten thousand yen! That's absurd!

moku moku   do something in silence; billow up*

- *Keiri buchō wa moku moku to shigoto o shite iru.*
  The accounting department chief is quietly getting on with his work.

mota mota   slow, inefficient; tardy

- *Chin'age no kōshō ga mota mota shite iru uchi ni, rōdō kumiai wa suto ni totsunyū shite shimatta.*
  While the wage negotiations dragged on, the union plunged into a strike.

mori mori   full of zest or ambition; work hard; eat hard*

- *Kyō wa mori mori hataraku zo, to jibun ni iikikasemashita.*
  "Today I'll really work hard," I vowed to myself.

yakimoki   anxious, on edge; impatient

- *Ōkii yushutsu chūmon ga mada happyō sarete inakatta node, kare wa yakimoki shite shirase o matte ita.*
  Because the big export order hadn't been announced yet, he was waiting on tenterhooks for the news.

nonbiri   sit back and relax, be calm; happy-go-lucky

- *Kare no jōshi wa ima shutchō chū na node nonbiri dekiru to omotte imasu.*
  He thinks he can sit back and relax because his boss is away on business right now.

norari kurari   laze around; beat around the bush, vague*

- *Jimusho de ichinichijū shinbun o yondari, kōhii o nondari shite norari kurari jikan o sugosu shain ga kanari iru.*

There are a fair number of employees who laze around all day, reading newspapers and drinking coffee.

nobi nobi   stretch out, relax, feel relieved

A Japanese bank has tied this phrase up with a British cartoon character who is always wandering around in a relaxed way and is very hard to find. The bank wants you to invest your money with them, which must imply that relaxing is no longer considered a bad thing.

- *Jimusho no erebētā ni notta shunkan ikkagetsu no natsu yasumi ga hajimatta nā to omotte, hontō ni nobi nobi shite tanoshii kimochi ni natta.*

  The second I got in the office elevator I thought, "I'm on holiday for a month!" and I felt really happy and relaxed.

Note that a homonym of this phrase written with different kanji means to delay something.

Deal Making and Money Making

These are phrases that are useful in the workplace, but I suspect many people find them equally applicable at home, particularly if there are teenage children about, who seem to strike some of the hardest bargains and make the most outrageous demands for funds.

gatchiri   careful with money; carefully do something; solidly, firmly*

- *Shinshachō no keiei ga gatchiri shite iru node, kotoshi no rieki wa kyonen no bai ni narimashita.*
  Because of the new president's careful management, this year's profits are double last year's.

gappo gappo   rake in money

- *Kenkō shokuhin ga saikin ninki ga dete iru node, ano shizen shokuryōhin gaisha wa gappo gappo mōkete imasu.*
  Because health foods have become popular recently, that natural food company is raking in money.

gappori   rake in money in one go, or lose it all at once

- *Kyonen kare wa kabu de gappori mōketa ga, kotoshi wa shotokuzei de motte ikareta.*
  Last year he made a killing on stocks, but this year taxes gobbled most of it up.

gabo gabo   rake in money; loose-fitting; gurgling sound*

- *Hontō ni ii seihin o hanbai sureba, o-kane wa gabo gabo haitte kuru yo.*
  If you market a really good product, the money will come rolling in.

72

gabotto   large profit, large loss

- *Kare wa mukashi kabu de gabotto mōketa.*
  In the past, he made a fortune in the stock market.

gun   striking progress; put strength into a single effort*

- *X-sha ga bōdai na waribiki o teikyō shita node, kōshō wa gun to kōka o ageta.*
  After Company X offered a huge discount, the negotiations were remarkably fruitful.

gun gun   vigorous, striking progress

- *Sono shinseihin no uriage wa gun gun nobite imasu.*
  Sales of the new product are growing remarkably.

sura sura   proceed smoothly, without a hitch; flow

- *Wagasha to X-sha no aida no shōgyō kyōryoku kyōtei no hanashi wa sura sura to matomatta.*
  The talks on a commercial-cooperation agreement between our company and Company X proceeded without a hitch.

zun zun   rapid progress or regression

- *Shijō chōsa no okage de kotoshi no uriage wa zun zun nobita.*
  Thanks to our market research, this year's sales have expanded rapidly.

sunnari   progress without a hitch; slender*

- *Sono mondai wa sunnari kaiketsu saremashita.*
  That problem was sorted out without a hitch.
- *Kodomo wa sunnari gakkō ni nare, tanoshigatte iru yō da.*

Our child has adjusted to school without a hitch and seems to be enjoying it.

soro soro   slow, gradual progress; about time to

This is a very useful phrase for easing your departure from friends or acquaintances, especially if you have a partner who is always reluctant to leave a party.

- *Sate, sore de wa soro soro kaerimashō.*
  Well, I guess we should begin to think about leaving.
- *Uriage no nobinayami de kaisha mo soro soro genkai da.*
  With our difficulty in increasing sales, the company will gradually go under.

giri giri   just in time or within the limit; rock bottom price; grating, grinding

- *Giri giri no jikan ni yōyaku nyūsatsu o oeta.*
  We delivered our bid at the last possible moment.

gossori   robbed clean; entirely, completely

- *Sono torihiki de wagasha wa gossori motte ikareta.*
  Our company was robbed clean in that transaction.

zaku zaku   money rolls in; rough weave; crunch

- *Nanimo shinakute mo, kare ni wa o-kane ga zaku zaku haitte kuru.*
  Even if he does nothing, the money comes rolling in.

jan jan   sell like hot cakes; lavish money on; receive lots of money; things occurring one after another; ring

- *Ano atarashii gēmu wa jan jan urete, mō urikiremashita.*
  That new game sold like hot cakes and it's already out of stock.

74

pon pon   sell like hot cakes; in rapid succession; clap hands; speak without reserve; popping corks*

- *Kono nyū moderu wa pon pon tobu yō ni urete imasu.*
  This new model is really selling fast.

meki meki   make marked progress; sell like hot cakes

- *Keiki ga sukoshi yoku natta node, ware ware no uriage mo meki meki agatta.*
  Since the business environment has improved a little, our sales figures have improved markedly.

don   large sum used in one go; boom; thud*

- *Tochi, kabu, sore ni aburae de, don to hyakuman doru ga tonde shimatta.*
  I used up a million dollars in one go, buying land, stocks, and oil paintings.

ton ton   be on par (e.g., a balance of revenue and expenditure); proceed smoothly; tapping, knocking

- *A-sha ga B-sha ni kyūshū sareta tōji wa ton ton datta shūshi ga, rainen no saishū son'eki de wa kuroji ni narisō da.*
  When Company A was bought by Company B its balance of revenue and expenditure was on par, but it is expected that end of term earnings next year will move it into the black.

pā   go down the drain, wasted effort; foolish

- *Sekaijū no fukeiki de, wagasha no tōshi wa pā ni natta.*
  In the world-wide recession, our company's investments went down the drain.

pappa   waste (money); suddenly and energetically

- *Ano hito wa kane sae areba, pappa to tsukatte shimau.*
  As long as he has money, he spends it heedlessly.

gata gata   be shaky; tremble; rattle; sudden decline; complain*

- *Songai baishōkin o haratte kara, kaisha no zaisei wa gata gata ni natta.*
  After paying compensation for damages, the company's financial position became shaky.

karappo   empty

- *Keibajō ni itte, saifu ga karappo ni natte shimatta.*
  I went to the race track and came back with an empty wallet.

suttenten   flat broke

- *Tochi no tōki ni o-kane o tsukaihatashite suttenten ni natte shimatta.*

He used up all his money on land speculation and is now penniless.

kyū kyū   hard up for money; tight (schedule); squeaky (shoes)

• *Kubi ni natte kara, seikatsu ni kyū kyū to shite iru.*
Since he lost his job, he's been leading a hand-to-mouth existence.

pii pii   in dire straits (financially); a high-pitched sound; chirp

• *Boku wa itsumo kane ga nakute pii pii shite iru.*
I'm always short of money and in dire straits.

· 5 ·
WINE, WOMEN, AND SONG

The first image that comes to mind when I hear the words "wine, women, and song" is Roppongi, the brash, vibrant entertainment district most frequented by foreigners in Tokyo. But Japanese nightlife as we know it now, with bar-hopping and dancing at discos, is still a fairly recent phenomenon. Most of the phrases in this section hark back to much earlier times, when "wine, women, and song" suggested something entirely different in Japan.

Wine

Saké has flowed freely in Japan from ancient times. Shrine festivals were always boisterous with the high spirits of intoxicated young men heaving the portable shrine, or *mikoshi,* through the streets in the precincts of the shrine. In a society mostly devoid of puritanical notions, drunkenness was hardly seen as a crime, and many indiscretions were excusable if it could be explained that the perpetrator had been drunk. In the post-war years, Japanese office workers easily made the transition from festival merriment to after-work drinking together, often to excess, as a way of enhancing the group spirit.

This is less the norm in Japan today. People still enjoy drinking together, but greater emphasis is placed on people's personal lives and the inevitable long commutes to work mean that people no longer want to spend so much time in bars, or recovering from getting drunk. A book I was reading recently on business protocol advises its readers to enjoy alcohol but to guard against having the drinking party end in a drunken mess. That having been said, there's no better way to unwind after a hard day and get to know your business colleagues or your Japanese friends than over a cold glass of your favorite brew.

Drinking

gabu gabu   gulp, guzzle

* *Ano hito wa biiru ga daisuki de maiban gabu gabu nonde imasu.*
  That fellow loves beer and tosses back large amounts every night.

gabo gabo   gurgling sound; loose-fitting; rake in money*

* *Mizu o nomisugite, i ga gabo gabo da.*
  My stomach makes an embarrassing gurgling noise whenever I drink too much water.

kara kara   parched; empty; laugh with a high-pitched voice; clatter*; very dry*

* *Yakyū no shiai de ōgoe de ōen shita tame nodo ga kara kara da.*
  Because I cheered loudly at the baseball game, my throat is dry and sore.

kyutto   gulp; tight; pinch

* *Mazu saisho ni kyutto ippai yattara, mūdo ga moriagatta.*
  After we first had a quick drink, the mood warmed up.

gui gui   drink vigorously, gulp; push or pull with all one's strength*
guitto   gulp down in one go; apply all one's strength at once*

* *Akira wa sake o gui gui nonde, satto nomiya o tachisatta.*
  Akira gulped down his saké and quickly left the bar.

kukū   drink in one gulp

Kukū describes the act of drinking in one gulp rather than the sound it makes.

- *Hiyazake o kukū to nomihoshita.*
  We drank up the cold saké at once.

gutto   gulp; concentrated action; feel strongly; pull forcefully

- *Burandē o gutto nomihoshita.*
  He quaffed a glass of brandy.

gubiri gubiri   guzzle

- *Tonari no hito wa masu de gubiri gubiri to yatte iru.*
  The man next to me is guzzling saké from a wooden cup.

goku goku   gulping sound in throat, glug glug

- *Mōretsu na atsusa no naka de tsumetai mizu o goku goku nonda node, totemo umakatta.*
  We were enjoying the cold water as we gulped it down in the terrible heat.

kokun   gulp down; drop head suddenly (e.g., when falling asleep)

- *Suzuki-san wa watashi ga tsukutta umeshu o kokun to oto o tatete nomikonda.*
  With a gulping sound, Mr. Suzuki swallowed the plum wine I'd made.

chibi chibi   small sips; nibble; little by little

- *Akiko wa chibi chibi to oishii nihonshu o nonde iru.*
  Akiko is taking small sips of the delicious saké.

toku toku   sound or act of pouring a liquid; speak proudly

- *Toku toku to koppu ni uisukii o tsuida.*
  He poured the whiskey into a glass.

pon   pull out a cork; without hesitation, casually; pat (e.g., on the back)

pon pon   popping corks; in rapid succession; clap hands; speak without reserve; sell like hot cakes*

- *Koruku no sen o pon to nuite oishii shanpan o nonda.*
  I popped the cork and drank the delicious champagne.

nami nami   overflowing, brimful

- *Shachō wa ōki na sakazuki ni nami nami sosogareta sake o hitoiki ni nomimashita.*
  In one go the president drank the large cup filled to the brim with saké.

doppuri   in too deep; steeped or deeply immersed in something (e.g., a bath or soy sauce)* (used with *tsukeru* or *tsukaru*)

- *Shiken ga owatta ato, sono daigakusei-tachi wa hotto shita sei ka, maiban sake ni doppuri tsukatta seikatsu o shite imashita.*
  After the exams were over, the university students felt relieved and spent every evening in a drunken stupor.

Getting Drunk

horotto   tipsy; something light and small falling (e.g., a tear);

slight stimulation of the senses; feel pleasure or sympathy; nice bitter taste*

- *Kare wa shin'yū to nonde iru uchi ni horotto shite kita.*
  While drinking with his good friend, he gradually began to feel tipsy.

fura fura   become unsteady, waver; feel dizzy

- *Kanojo wa sakezuki to iu wake de wa nai node, ippai de mo nomu to fura fura ni naru.*
  She's not a drinker. After only one drink she becomes unsteady.

yoro yoro   stagger; lose one's balance*

- *Sannin no sarariiman wa yoro yoro to tachiagatte kara, kanjō o haratta.*
  The three office workers staggered to their feet and paid their bill.

muka muka   feel nauseous; very angry

- *Pātii de nomisugita tame kaerimichi mune ga muka muka shita.*
  I drank too much at the party and felt nauseous on the way home.

gē gē   retch, vomit

- *Bōnenkai de iroiro na shurui no sake o nonda node, densha no naka de gē gē to haite shimatta.*
  I drank too many kinds of alcohol at the year-end party and threw up in the train afterward.

gero gero   vomit continuously

- *Nomiya no waki no semai roji ni gero gero yatte iru otoko wa ōzei ita.*
  The alley by the tavern was crowded with men throwing up.

guden guden   get drunk (and not remember)

- *Sumiko no otto wa maiban guden guden ni yopparatte kaette kuru.*
  Sumiko's husband comes home dead drunk every night.

bero bero   dead drunk; lick vigorously (more heavily than *pero pero*)*

- *Mada yoi no kuchi da to iu noni, kare wa sude ni bero bero ni natte ita.*
  Although it was still early evening, he was already plastered.

meta meta   smashed; bushed*

- *Yūbe boku wa takusan nomisugite meta meta datta.*
  I drank too much last night and was really smashed.

mero mero   drunk; discouraged; controlled by one's wife

- *Mero mero ni yopparatte, eki kara uchi made arukenakatta.*
  He got dead drunk and couldn't walk from the station to his house.

Women (and Men)

Japan's warrior-dominated feudal era left Japanese women entirely subordinate to men except at home, where they did continue to have some authority over the raising of the children and financial affairs. There are many colorful onomatopoeic phrases describing female appearance and personality. Far fewer exist to describe masculine traits, except for expressions of strength, which I have included in the section on sumo. I assume that this is because men have long been in the habit of making observations about women, but women have been far more reticent about discussing men. Things are changing, but it will take time before new attitudes show up as permanent expressions in the language.

Occasionally, expressions that mainly describe masculine traits do crop up in reference to women. When the engagement of the Crown Prince was announced, I wondered how the media would describe his fiancée, a well-educated career woman named Masako Owada. A certain amount of reserve was inevitable, in view of the lofty status to which the young woman would soon be elevated. One popular magazine chose the headline, "Prince to Wed Superlady." They weren't quite ready to refer to her as a super*woman* (No Superwomen Please, We're Japanese). A former ambassador describing Miss Owada used the phrase *dō dō,* which usually means imposing or majestic and dignified, hardly the traits of a traditional bride-to-be. This phrase can also refer to a woman who can hold her own with men.

Personality

Desirable personality traits seem to be pretty much the same the world over. But if you try to picture in your mind's eye female personifications of these phrases, don't be too surprised if stereotypes of Japanese women drift into view.

assari   easygoing, openhearted; light, delicate (flavor)*

• *Kanojo wa assari shite iru kara, boku no suki na taipu no onna no ko da.*
   She's openhearted, the kind of girl I like.

iji iji   introverted, inhibited

- *Kirei na ko da kedo, iji iji shita seikaku de unzari da.*
  She's a pretty girl, but I can't stand her being so introverted.

iso iso   light-hearted and cheerful; looking forward to something, eager

- *Wakai futarizure wa iso iso to dēto ni dekaketa.*
  The young couple set off eagerly on their date.

uki uki   eager, light-hearted, cheerful

- *Shōtengai no hokōsha tengoku wa uki uki shita wakamono de nigiwatta.*
  The pedestrian-only shopping area was crowded with light-hearted young people.

uji uji   wishy-washy, indecisive

- *Kanojo wa uji uji to mayotte, resutoran de ryōri o chūmon suru noni, jippun ijō kakaru.*
  She's so indecisive that it takes her over ten minutes to choose her food in a restaurant.

odo odo   uptight, tense, nervous; lacking self-confidence

- *Itsumo odo odo shite ite, ittai dō shita no?*
  You're always so uptight. What on the earth is the matter?

gasa gasa   rough, insensitive; noisy, rustle; dried out

- *Kare wa gasa gasa shita kanji na node, issho ni iru no wa gaman dekinai.*
  I can't stand to be with him because he's so insensitive.

kachi kachi   stubborn; hard; ticking; click-clack of wooden clappers

- *Kare wa ganko de atama ga kachi kachi na node nani o shite mo tanoshimenai.*
  He's so inflexible and stubborn, he can't enjoy anything.

gami gami   nagging

- *Asa kara ban made gami gami iwareru okage de, boku wa nanimo dekinai.*
  Because you nag me all day long I can't do anything.
- *Gami gami iu tsuma kara nigeru tame ni, pachinkoya ni itta.*
  I went to the pachinko parlor to get away from my wife's nagging.

karari   cheerful; clatter; clear, dry*; crisp*

- *Kanojo wa karari to shita seikaku na node dare ni de mo sukareru.*
  She has a cheerful disposition and is well-liked by everyone.

kyoto kyoto   jittery, look around nervously

- *Kare wa kyoto kyoto atari o mimawashite ochitsuki no nai yōsu de heya ni haitta.*
  He looked around and entered the room nervously.

kunya kunya   bend easily, irresolute

- *Kunya kunya shite ite kikotsu no nai otoko da.*
  He's an irresolute, spineless person.

kose kose   fussy; narrow, cramped

- *Kare wa kose kose shita hito de itsumo mentsu ni kodawaru no desu.*
  He's a fussy person, always worrying about losing face.

kochi kochi   inflexible, stubborn; tense; rock hard*

- *Ano hito wa atama ga kochi kochi na node ittan kimeta koto wa naka naka kaerarenai.*
  He's an inflexible fellow. Once he decides something, he doesn't easily change his mind.

sappari   fresh and simple, open; not at all; refreshing*

- *Kanojo wa sappari shita kishō de chōdo jibun no konomi ni aimasu.*
  She has an open, fresh personality, just the way I like it.

saba saba   carefree, detached; fresh, neat; feel relieved

- *Kare wa totemo saba saba shita otoko de, guchi ya uramigoto o itta koto ga nai.*
  He's so easygoing, never grumbling or complaining.

sarari   easygoing, carefree; smooth action, slide; fresh and dry*

- *Kanojo wa sarari to shita seikaku da kara tsukiaiyasui.*
  It's nice to know her because she's so easygoing.

shikkari   steady, responsible, firm; sufficient

- *Kondo no gārufurendo wa shikkari shita hito no yō desu ne.*
  Your new girlfriend seems a steady sort of person.

shittori   tranquil, placid, pleasantly calm and elegant; moist*

- *Bijin de wa nai ni shite mo, shittori to ochitsuite iru ko da.*
  Even if she isn't a beauty, she's a calm, tranquil girl.

jime jime   melancholy, depressed; dark, gloomy; damp*

- *Kanojo wa itsumo kurai jime jime shita hyōjō o shite iru.*
  She always has a dark, melancholy look.

shā shā   brazen; shower, spray

- *Kanojo wa shā shā to itsumo nan de mo shirabakureru ga, hontō wa nan de mo yoku shitte iru no desu.*
  She always puts on a big act like she doesn't know anything, but she actually knows everything.

tsun, tsūn   standoffish; pointed; pungent, stinging*

- *Kanojo wa iya ni tsun to sumashite iru kanji de tsumetai ne.*
  She seems cold and conceited, doesn't she?

toge toge   harsh, prickly, thorny; sarcastic

- *Sō toge toge shita iikata o suru na.*
  Don't be so harsh.

nuke nuke   brazen

- *Kare wa itsumo nuke nuke to uso o tsuku.*
  He's always telling barefaced lies.
- *Sono kurai nuke nuke to shita koto ga ieru hito wa sōtō no tanuki da.*
  A fellow who can talk as brazenly as that is crafty.

nechi nechi   be a pest, tenacious (in a bad way); stick firmly*

- *Aitsu wa nechi nechi shita otoko da!*
  That guy's such a pest!

fuwa fuwa   frivolous; giddy; soft, buoyant, fluffy, light*

- *Emi wa fuwa fuwa shita ko de shinrai dekinai.*
  Emi's a frivolous girl, and I can't depend on her.

muttsuri   silent, tight-lipped; glum

- *Warui otoko de wa nai ga itsumo muttsuri oshidamatte iru node, tsukiainikui no desu.*
  He's not a bad person, but because he's always so quiet he's hard to relate to.

moji moji   fidget; hesitatingly

- *Wakai dansei kyōin no mae ni deru to, ano futari no onna no ko wa itsumo issho ni moji moji shite iru.*
  Those two girls always fidget together in front of the young male teacher.

91

Appearance and Behavior

I think these phrases suggest a distinct bias in Japanese in favor of plump, girlish types over thin, lavishily dressed mannequin types.

kichin   smart, stylish, organized

- *Kanojo no yō ni kichin to kikonasu onna wa metta ni inai.*
  One rarely sees a woman dressed as stylishly as she.

gisu gisu   very thin; cold (personality or atmosphere)

- *Kanojo wa se ga takaku, gisu gisu shita kanji no josei da.*
  She's a tall, angular woman.

keba keba   lavish, heavy, gaudy

- *Keba keba shita keshō wa kanojo ni niawanai.*
  Heavy make-up doesn't suit her.
- *Kinjo no atarashii pachinkoya wa zōka de keba keba to kazaritsukerarete ite, kirai da.*
  The new neighborhood pachinko parlor is decorated gaudily with artificial flowers. I hate it.

gotsu gotsu   rough or durable (body type); sound of two hard things banging into one another

- *Kare wa karada ga ōgara de, gotsu gotsu shite iru ga kao wa waruku wa nai.*
  He has got a large build and is a bit roughhewn, but is not bad looking.

gote gote   gaudy; thick and heavy; say over and over again

- *Hosutesu wa taitei kao o gote gote nuritakutte iru.*

Women working in hostess bars often heavily paint their faces with make-up.

koro koro   plump; ring of a bell; rolling; giggling; cricket's chirp*

* *Kanojo wa koro koro futotte ite, kawaii ne.*
She's plump and cute.

shanari shanari   gracefully; haughtily

* *Moderu ga shanari shanari to tōjō shite, atarashii fasshon o hirō shita.*
The models paraded across the stage showing the new fashions.

jara jara   overdone finery; clatter, jangle

* *Kanojo wa itsumo akusesarii o jara jara sasete iru.*
She always overdoes her accessories.

sukkiri   simple, perky; trim; refreshing

- *Kare to kanojo wa futari tomo itsumo sukkiri to shita fukusō o shite iru.*
  Both he and she always dress simply but fashionably.

surari   long and slender; smooth unbroken movement, nimbly

- *Se ga surari to shita onna ga kuruma kara orita.*
  A tall, slender woman got out of the car.

zunguri   short and fat

- *Ano bijin wa zunguri shita otoko to kekkon shita.*
  That beautiful woman married a short, fat man.

sunnari   slender; progress without a hitch*

- *Kare wa sunnari shita karadatsuki no gārufurendo o achi kochi tsurete aruku.*
  He takes his shapely girlfriend with him wherever he goes.

chima chima   fine, pinched features; neatly

- *Kanojo wa mehana ga chima chima shite iru.*
  She has pinched features.

chiri chiri   crinkly, frizzy; jingle, continual small ring; shrink in fear

- *Kanojo wa pāma o kakete, kaminoke ga chiri chiri ni natte iru.*
  She's had a perm and her hair is all crinkly.

chara chara   dress up too much; flirt; jangle; flatter; sexy; overdone finery

* *Chara chara mekashikonde iru ano onna wa, kitto bā no hosutesu da.*
  Judging from how she's dressed, that woman must be a bar hostess.

teka teka   shiny, brightly

* *Kanojo wa teka teka shita doresu o kite shumi ga warui.*
  She has bad taste, getting dressed up so gaudily.

debu debu   fat, flabby

* *Kanojo wa itsumo poteto chippu o tabete iru node debu debu futotte kita.*
  She's constantly eating potato chips, so she's grown really fat.

dō dō   majestic, dignified; capable of holding one's own

* *Masako-san wa nannin mo no otoko no hito-tachi no mae de mo dō dō to giron suru koto ga dekiru.*

95

Masako is capable of holding her own in a discussion with several men.

nopperi   flat and plain (face or body)

- *Sono shimai no kao wa ryōhō tomo nopperi shite kurai.*
  Both of those sisters' faces are plain and expressionless.

buku buku   swollen and fat; swish fluid in one's mouth; sound of bubbling*

- *Toshi o toru ni tsurete, buku buku futoridasu.*
  As you get older, you tend to get flabby.

fukkura   plump; swollen and soft (e.g., a pillow)

- *Ano fukkura shita kao no musume wa kawaii desu.*
  That round-faced young girl is charming.

boin   busty; forcefully punch or kick

Foreign girls are indiscriminately described as *boin* by some Japanese men.

- *Mari wa boin na node, bikini ga niaimasu.*
  Because Mari is well-endowed, she looks nice in a bikini.

pocha pocha   chubby and cute; roly-poly
potchari   nicely plump, chubby and cute; splash

- *Sono potchari to kawaii josei wa disuko de hataraite iru.*
  That cute plump girl works at the disco.

botteri   large, fat, fleshy, heavy

- *Ano botteri shita karadatsuki no otoko wa boku no bosu da.*
  That heavy-set man is my boss.

bote bote   grossly fat

- *Watashi no rūmumeito wa bote bote ni futotte iru.*
  My roommate is very obese.

mutchiri   plump, fleshy, full-bodied

- *Kanojo wa mutchiri shita yawarakai hada o arawani shita.*
  She revealed her soft plump flesh.

mun mun   sultry; humid*

- *Sake, ongaku, soshite nekki de mun mun shite iru tokoro da.*
  It's a place for wine, music, and an atmosphere heavy with sultry promise.

yuttari   mellow, carefree; leisurely; spacious

- *Kare wa yuttari shita yatsu de, metta ni okoranai.*
  He's mellow and almost never gets angry.

yore yore   wrinkled or worn-out clothing

- *Kanojo wa yasashii ko da ga, itsumo yore yore ni natta sukāto o darashinaku haite iru.*
  She's a sweet girl, but she's always wearing sloppy, worn-out skirts.

Relationships

For a long time, romance and social mixing could be found only in the amusement quarters. Even twenty years ago, dating among the young was almost non-existent, and Japanese women habitually walked a step or two behind their male companions. Times are

changing and phrases that once had a negative connotation are now frequently used in a positive sense.

icha icha   showing affection in public

- *Saishū densha wa icha icha shite iru wakai kappuru de ippai datta.*
  The last train was full of young couples caressing each other.

gunya gunya   soft and weak

- *Kare wa ano bijin ni gunya gunya ni honenuki ni sarete shimatta.*
  That beautiful woman has made him weak and spineless.

shikkuri   get along well (usually used in the negative sense)

- *Sono kappuru wa saikin shikkuri itte inai.*
  That couple has not been getting along well recently.

zuki zuki   heartache; continual painful throb*

- *Sono mukashi no koibito o omoidasu tabi ni, zuki zuki to iu kokoro no uzuki o oboemasu.*
  Whenever I think of that old flame, I remember my heartache.

zuta zuta   heartbroken; cut in ribbons, shredded

- *Kare no iede ga watashi no kokoro o zuta zuta ni shita.*
  When he left me, it cut my heart to pieces.

zokkon   deeply involved, crazy about

- *Ken wa Bābii ni zokkon horekonde iru.*
  Ken's madly in love with Barbie.

chu, chutto   kiss; chirp

- *Dare mo mite inai toki ni kawaii kanojo ga boku ni chutto shite kureta.*
  While no one was looking, the cute girl gave me a kiss on the cheek.

dere dere   mess around, flirt; be turned to putty by someone

- *Kare no toshi de jogakusei to dere dere shite mo ii to omotte iru no darō ka?*
  Does he think it's okay to mess around with schoolgirls at his age?

hoya hoya   fresh state (for both people and things); food hot from the oven*

- *Ano tanoshisō na wakai danjo. Shinkon hoya hoya deshō.*
  That happy young couple—I suppose they're newlyweds.

beta beta   a couple falling all over each other; pasted, sticky*

- *Hitomae de beta beta shite iru wakai kappuru wa chotto hatameiwaku da.*
  Young couples falling all over each other in public are a little annoying.

bettari   stuck firmly, be very close; daub, coat; sit in one spot without moving

- *Kanojo ni aitai kedo ano sukii no kyōshi ga bettari kuttsuite iru.*
  I want to meet her, but that ski instructor is always with her.

Song

Western music first arrived in Japan with the Portuguese missionaries in the 16th century, only to disappear again with the expulsion of the missionaries in the early 17th century. It wasn't until much later, in the years just prior to the onset of the Meiji Restoration, that interest in western music was rekindled. Of course, the Japanese have always had their own musical tradition, covering a wide range of genres from the ancient court music, or *gagaku*, to the rousing drum music and dance rhythms that are so much a part of summer festivals. Not surprisingly, there are many phrases to describe the sound of clanging, beating, and ringing, but very few that relate to singing or serenading.

kan kan   high clear ring, clang; very angry*; blazing sun or heat*
gan gan   dull heavy clang; do something vigorously*; throbbing headache*

- *Kōji genba kara gan gan to kinzoku o tataku oto ga hibikiatatte iru.*
  The sound of clanging metal echoed from the construction site.
- *Kan kan to kane o narashite kinjo no hito ni kaji o shiraseta.*
  I warned everyone in my neighborhood that there was a fire by ringing a bell.

101

chirin chirin   tinkle, jingle, jangle (louder than *chiri chiri*, with pauses between sounds)

- *Kodomo wa jitensha no beru o chirin chirin to narashita.*
  The child was jingling his bicycle bell continuously.
- *Engawa de yūsuzumi o shite iru to, fūrin ga chirin chirin to natte ita.*
  The wind bell tinkled in the breeze as we enjoyed the evening cool on the verandah.

chin chin   ding ding; kettle whistling; (dog) stands up
chiin chiin   ding dong

- *Chiin chiin to kane o narashite o-bōsan ga o-kyō o tonae-hajimeta.*
  After ringing the bell, the Buddhist priest began to intone the prayers.

This phrase, in combination with *don don* produces the expression *chindonya*, or ding-dong band. This group of three or four men and women, dressed rather haphazardly in traditional garb, parade through neighborhoods with drums and noisemakers creating a din in order to advertise special sales or events.

don don   rat-a-tat-tat, roll of drums; speak out; advance rapidly; increasingly

- *Tarō wa matsuri no taiko o don don to ikioi yoku tataite iru.*
  Taro is beating the festival drum loudly.
- *Ano yūshū na gakusei wa itsumo don don shitsumon suru.*
  That excellent student always fires questions one after another.

bū bū   blow a horn, toot; human griping about something; pig's grunt or snort*
pū pū   blow a horn (a higher pitched sound than *bū bū*)

- *Seinen ga fuku toranpetto wa pū pū to naru bakari de naka naka jōtatsu shinai.*
  That young man is blowing the trumpet but he hasn't improved.

pen pen   pluck a samisen

- *Kirei na geisha ga Kyōto no ryōtei de shamisen o pen pen to kakinarashite ita.*
  A pretty geisha was strumming a samisen in the Kyoto restaurant.

boron boron   pluck or strum a stringed instrument (e.g., a bass)
poron poron   pluck or strum a stringed instrument (e.g., a guitar or a harp); strike piano keys

- *Kare ga kanaderu poron poron to iu gitā no oto wa kanashii kimochi ni saseta.*
  The sound of his guitar strumming made me sad.

rō rō   singing or reciting in a loud, clear voice

- *Kanojo wa dokushōkai de utsukushii koe de rō rō to utatta.*
  She sang in a loud, clear, beautiful voice at her recital.

· 6 ·
SUMO

Sumo is currently enjoying a huge revival of popularity among the Japanese. For many years it languished in the shadow of baseball, the modern, international sport. Foreigners living in Japan have always been fascinated by sumo. I think it is solely because the sport is so exotic, with its enormous, overweight wrestlers done up in their unique form of undress. There is a lot to learn about sumo, and a good number of English language sources exist to satisfy our curiosity.

The importance of tradition and ceremony to the popularity of sumo cannot be denied, but I think what really interests us now about the sport are the personalities involved. If Japan is the nation of groups, then sumo is the sport of individuals. There are the foreign strong men, struggling to make their way in a sport that does not welcome them. There is the cute and popular duo of Wakanohana and Takanohana, latest in the line of a famous sumo family. Twenty years ago I was a fan of their father, urging him on to victory tournament after tournament. The David and Goliath contests delight us, particularly when the smaller of the two wrestlers manages to win by a stunning use of technique or artifice. We watch with sadness as formerly great wrestlers begin to decline in strength with age. We worry if one of our favorites misses a tournament because of an injury or sickness. In short, we grow to love the big guys and feel we almost know them, as we identify with their struggles.

When you watch sumo on television, listen for the onomato- poeic phrases the announcer uses to describe the action. Like in the west, there is an art to the commentary in the long breaks between matches and during the bursts of frenzied activity. If you know several of these phrases and the names of sumo techniques, the reporting is surprisingly easy to understand.

The Wrestlers

Most commentary on sumo wrestlers concerns their strength, but truly great ones, like the retired grand champions Taiho and Chiyonofuji, are also expected to be dignified and almost regal in their bearing.

ottori   lordly, composed; big-hearted, generous

- *Chiyonofuji wa karadatsuki no yoi rikishi de, ottori shita yokozuna datta.*
  Chiyonofuji was a well-built wrestler and a regal grand champion.

gashitto   strongly built

- *Sumōtori ni naru tame ni wa, karadatsuki ga gashitto shite iru koto ga nani yori taisetsu da.*
  To become a sumo wrestler there's no substitute for having a firmly built body.

gasshiri   very solidly built, massive

- *Kondo no makuuchi no shinrikishi wa taikaku ga gasshiri shita wakamono de, kitto hayaku san'yaku ni agaru deshō.*
  The new senior-grade wrestler is a very solidly built youngster who should rise quickly to the top ranks.

kori kori   firm muscle; stiff (shoulders); rubbery*

- *Mainoumi wa karada ga chiisakute mo, kori kori to kobutori no jōbusō na rikishi da.*
  Even though Mainoumi is small, he is firmly built and appears strong.

doshi doshi   walk heavily, stamp; continue one after another; not hold back

- *Sekitori ga doshi doshi to aruite, nyūjō shite kita.*
  The sumo wrestlers came into the stadium walking heavily.

dosshiri   dignified, impressive; heavy

- *Mae no yokozuna Taihō wa kodomo ni ai sareta dosshiri shita jinbutsu da.*
  The former grand champion Taiho is an impressive figure, loved by children.

nosshi nosshi   walk heavily; walk leisurely

- *Konishiki wa karada ga taihen omoi sumōtori de nosshi nosshi to aruku.*
  Konishiki is a very weighty wrestler with a heavy, lumbering gait.

piritto   sharpness, freshness

- *Yokozuna ga keikoba de nanika piritto shinai no wa kigakari de aru.*
  It's a troubling sign that the grand champion lacked sharpness during training.

funya funya   lose one's edge; flaccid, limp, squishy

- *Haru basho mae, kekkon shita bakari no Konishiki wa funya funya datta.*
  Before the Spring Tournament, the newly wed Konishiki had lost his edge.

The Matches

With the slamming of bodies into the sand and the slaps and thuds as giant torsos collide, sumo matches are rich in onomatopoeic phrases to describe the action.

appu appu   struggle desperately; gasp for air (while drowning); up to one's neck in debt

- *Kotozakura wa appu appu no kakkō de dohyō no soto ni oshidasareta.*
  Struggling hard, Kotozakura was pushed out of the ring.

gatto   seize, hold with strength

- *Ryō ōzeki wa gatto hidari yotsu de butsukariatta.*
  The two champions quickly seized each other with left-handed holds.

gatchiri   firmly, solidly; carefully do something; careful with money*

- *Konishiki wa mazu migi uwate o tsukande, soshite hidari no shitate mo gatchiri tsukande aite o gutto hikitsuketa.*
  Konishiki first got a right-handed outside grip, then a firm left-handed underhand grip with which he forcefully pulled up his opponent.

gappuri   lock together

- *Hatsu yūshō no basho ni Takanohana wa donna taipu no aite ni mo gappuri no yotsuzumō de shōbu shita.*
  In the first tournament he won, Takanohana came to grips with each opponent, no matter what sort of wrestler he was.

gatsun bang

- *Musashimaru ga gatsun to morote tsuki de semekonda.*
  Thrusting with both hands, Musashimaru attacked with a bang.

gan gan do something vigorously; dull heavy clang*; throbbing headache*

- *Sumōtori wa basho mae ni gan gan keiko shite ita.*
  The wrestler was training vigorously before the tournament.

gyutto push or squeeze with force

- *Rikishi wa saigo no shunkan ni gyutto semekonde yūshō shita.*
  The winning wrestler attacked with great force at the last minute.

gui gui push or pull with all one's strength; drink vigorously, gulp*
guitto apply all one's strength at once; gulp down in one go*

- *Takanohana wa shidai ni gui gui to Konishiki o oshidashita.*
  Using all his might, Takanohana gradually pushed Konishiki out of the ring.
- *Musashimaru wa aite o dohyō kara guitto oshidashita.*
  All at once Musashimaru powerfully pushed his opponent out of the ring.

gun put strength into a single effort; striking progress*

- *Wakai rikishi ga gun to oshite mo ōzeki o ugokasenakatta.*
  Even though the young wrestler pushed with all his strength, he couldn't move the champion.

gon   bang (heads); ring

- *Sekitori dōshi ga gon to atama o butsukeatta ga, saiwai ni kega wa nakatta.*
  The wrestlers banged heads, but fortunately they didn't get hurt.

gorori   (heavy object) rolling; lying awkwardly

- *Akinoshima wa shitate hineri de Konishiki o gorori to ōten saseta.*
  Akinoshima threw Konishiki on his side with an underarm twist.

jikkuri   carefully; talk things over; think carefully*

- *Muzukashii aite o jikkuri to semete sekitori wa yōyaku shiroboshi o agemashita.*
  The wrestler was careful as he attacked his difficult opponent and won the bout.

suten, sutten   tumble and fall

- *Ano rikishi wa yoku ganbatta ga, inasarete suten to koronda.*
  That wrestler fought hard, but his attack was dodged and he tumbled and fell.

zuru zuru   slowly slip backward; sound of a heavy object being dragged; lose repeatedly; slurp*

- *Kasugafuji wa aite no rikishi no tosshin de zuru zuru to kōtai shite dohyō no soto e oshidasareta.*
  Kasugafuji slid backward due to his opponent's charge and was pushed from the ring.

taji taji   be thrown off balance; cannot hold one's own*

- *Sekiwake no tsuppari de taji taji to nari, ushiro e sagatta.*
  Thrown off balance by the junior champion's thrusting attack, he staggered backwards.

daddatto   abruptly do something

- *Kirishima wa aite rikishi o daddatto ikki ni yori-kirimashita.*
  In one stroke, Kirishima pushed his opponent out of the ring.

dokatto   heavy fall

- *Mitoizumi wa Tochinowaka ga yorikitta toki, dokatto taorekonda.*
  Mitoizumi fell heavily when Tochinowaka forced him out of the ring by his belt.

dokan   slam (of a collision)

- *Futari no rikishi wa tachiai de dokan to butsukarimashita.*
  The two wrestlers slammed into each other at the initial charge.

dosatto   fall with a thud

- *Aite ga dosatto taoreta toki, Kirishima wa hoshi o gobu ni modoshita.*
  Kirishima returned to an even number of wins and losses when his opponent hit the dirt.

dosun dosun   stamp in succession; lumber

- *Rikishi wa dosun dosun to shiko o fumu.*
  The wrestler stamps the ring repeatedly.

bashitto   slap; firm decisive action

- *Sekiwake wa aite ni bashitto harite o kutte, ashi ga tsuite ikezu, tsuchi ga tsukimashita.*
  When the junior champion was slapped forcefully by his opponent, he lost his footing and hit the dirt.

don   thud; boom; large sum used in one go*

- *Tachiai de ryō rikishi wa don to butsukatta.*
  When the two wrestlers sprang forward at the start of the bout, they collided with a thud.

patto   vivid lively state (but used negatively to mean dull); sudden rapid action; scatter

- *Yokozuna Hokutoumi ga intai o happyō suru mae no basho no seiseki wa patto shinakatta.*
  Before he announced his retirement, grand champion Hokutoumi's results in the tournaments were lackluster.

putsutto, putsun   sound of a tense object being cut or broken; prick, pierce

- *Tsunahiki de tsuna ga putsutto kireta.*

  The rope snapped in the tug of war.

When Konishiki sustained his third loss in the January '92 tournament, a newspaper headline lamented, *"Konishiki, tsuna putsun,"* or, "the rope snapped," meaning that with that loss he wouldn't be promoted to grand champion rank after the tournament.

mitchiri   hard training

- *Sumōtori wa maibasho no mae ni, nanshūkan mo mitchiri kitaeraremasu.*

  Sumo wrestlers are put through hard training for many weeks before each tournament.

yoro yoro   lose one's balance; stagger*

- *Byōki de shutsujō shite ita rikishi wa aite no hatakikomi ni ashi ga yoro yoro shite, hayaku mo tsuchi ga tsukimashita.*

  The sick wrestler lost his balance from his opponent's assault and quickly hit the dirt.

un un   groan (with effort or pain); nod (in agreement)

No chapter on sumo would be complete without a word about Akebono's stunning defeat of Takahanada (now Takanohana) in the January, 1993 tournament, which led to his becoming the first foreign *yokozuna,* or grand champion.

- *Dohyō giwa de un un to koraeru Takahanada wa Akebono ni oshidasareta.*

  Struggling at the edge of the ring, Takahanada, with a groan, was thrown out.

114

· 7 ·
SICK AND TIRED

From time to time we all feel bad, whether we are actually sick, emotionally stretched to our limits, or just exhausted. The Japanese seem to have more than their share of aches and pains, and they have been able to avail themselves for centuries of a whole range of medicines and treatments to heal themselves. When *kanpō,* or the Chinese herbal medicines, acupuncture, and moxibustion could not cure their ills, they turned to *ranpō,* which first meant Dutch medicine and later came to mean Western medicine in general. Today, they also consume a huge quantity of vitamin and stamina drinks, just to get them through their long, exhausting days of work or study.

Sickness and Pain

One of the first words my Japanese teachers taught me was *netsu,* or fever. Every language emphasizes whatever its speakers are most concerned about, and I remember thinking that the Japanese must be preoccupied with their health and symptoms for our teachers to think it necessary to teach us so soon about illness. I still enjoy discussing health problems because twenty years ago my teachers made me something of an expert on the subject.

You will find the following phrases invaluable if you suddenly become sick and have to describe your symptoms to a Japanese doctor. Or perhaps, you may just want to discuss symptoms in conversation with a good friend.

gan gan throbbing headache; dull heavy clang*; do something vigorously*

• *Atama ga gan gan wareru yō ni itamimasu.*
  I have a splitting headache.

gikutto   suddenly hurt (one's back); be startled

- *Omoi hon o mochiageyō to shita toki, koshi ga gikutto natte ugokenaku natta.*
  When I tried to lift the heavy books, I felt a sudden pain in my lower back and couldn't move.

kiri kiri   sharp continuous pain; so busy you seem to be spinning*

- *Shigoto ga tamaru to, itsumo i ga kiri kiri itamu.*
  When work accumulates, I get stomach aches.

gura gura   loose; fickle; rickety; tremor; boil*

- *Shinikuen o nagaku hōtte oku to, ha ga gura gura ni naru.*
  If you don't do anything about your gum inflammation for a long time, your teeth will become loose.
- *Ano hito no kangae wa gura gura shite ite, ate ni naranai.*
  We can't rely on him because he is fickle.

gessori   look emaciated, haggard

- *Shibaraku awanai uchi ni, ano hito wa gessori yasete shimatta.*
  He's grown terribly thin during the time since I last met him.

gohon gohon   cough loudly

- *Zensoku no kanja wa gohon gohon to sekikonda.*
  The asthma patient had a coughing fit.

shiku shiku   dull pain; sob, cry (softly)

- *Ha ga shiku shiku shite, nemurenai.*
  I can't sleep because my tooth is aching.

jin, jiin   pins and needles; feel like you are going to cry; ringing vibration; numbing cold*

* *Atama o nagurare, jiin to itami ga hashitte ki o ushinatta.*
  When I was struck in the head, the pain was piercing and I lost consciousness.

zuki zuki   continual painful throb; heartache*
zukin   one sharp pain; feel a sharp pang of guilt
zukin zukin   continual throbbing pain (heavier than *zuki zuki*)

* *Asa kara ban made atama ga zuki zuki itanda.*
  My head ached continually from morning to night.

daku daku   perspire or bleed heavily; be very nervous

* *Kōtsū jiko no higaisha wa daku daku to chi o nagashite byōin ni hakobikomareta.*
  Bleeding profusely from the traffic accident, the victim was taken to the hospital.

doki doki   heart pounds

* *Undō shita ato wa shinzō ga doki doki kokyū ga hā hā shite, shibaraku kuchi mo kikenai.*
  After I exercise, my heart pounds, I puff and pant, and I can't speak for a while.

torotto   dull eyes; syrupy, glutinous; sleep lightly for a short period*; melt in your mouth*

* *Me ga torotto shite kita yo. Kitto nemui no da to omou.*
  Your eyes are dull. I'm sure you're sleepy.

hii hii   scream in pain

- *Hashigo kara ochite, ude no hone ga oreta toki, hii hii himei o ageta.*
  When she fell off the ladder and broke her arm, she screamed in pain.

piri piri   prickling pain; rip; blow a whistle; nervous; spicy food (more spicy that *hiri hiri*)*

- *Kōtsū jiko no ato, kizu ga piri piri itanda.*
  After the car accident, her wound was very painful.

pin pin   healthy; twang; strained; pull hard

- *Kare wa shujutsu no ato mo tassha de pin pin shite iru.*
  After his operation, he's as fit as a fiddle.

pokkuri   suddenly die; fragile

- *"Dare ni mo meiwaku o kakezu pokkuri shinitai" to kanojo wa itte ita.*
  "I want to die without causing anyone any trouble," she said.

muzu muzu   itchy; be itching to; feel anxious or impatient*

- *Ashi no yubi no aida ga muzu muzu kayui. Mizumushi no sei deshō.*
  The skin between my toes is itching. I wonder if it's athlete's foot.

Anger and Complaints

Feeling bad isn't always caused by illness. Sometimes what we have to put up with simply becomes too much for us, and this seems to be more true in Japanese cities than anywhere else. Everywhere we go there are crowds of people. It can take hours to escape from most major Japanese cities, and twice as long to get back. No wonder city dwellers often feel irritated.

It is interesting to note that these phrases usually have another meaning that is completely different from the expression of irritation or anger by which they are grouped here, such as disorder, a flash of heat or light, stabbing, a clanging sound, or a strong odor. These other meanings are often easy to associate with angry feelings, or the urge to complain.

ira ira   irritated, on edge

- *Kodomo no yakamashii koe ni wa ira ira suru.*
  The children's noisy voices irritate me.

gata gata   complain; rattle; tremble; sudden decline; be shaky*

- *Gata gata iwazu ni, hayaku heya o katazukenasai.*
  Clean up your room quickly, and no complaining.

katto   fly into a rage; thump, bang; sudden heat or light

- *Otto ga sono ban mata osoku natte kaette toki, katto natta.*
  When my husband was late again that night, I lost my temper.

kakka   burn with rage; blush; hot sensation; continuous heat or light*

- *Sono hidoi uwasa o kiita toki, hara ga tatte kao ga kakka to akaku natta.*
  When I heard that terrible rumor, my face became red with rage.

kari kari   worked up; crunchy, crisp*

- *Sō kari kari suru na yo.*

Don't get so worked up.

kan kan very angry; clang, high clear ring*; blazing sun or heat*

- *Seito ga mata shukudai o yatte konakatta node, sensei wa kan kan ni natta.*
  The teacher flew into a rage because once again his pupils hadn't completed their homework.

guzu guzu complain; sniffle; dillydally, make slow progress*

- *Kare no okusan wa itsumo kane no koto de guzu guzu itte iru.*
  His wife is always complaining about money.

gucha gucha complain; messy; chew, suck; mushy and wet*

- *Aitsu wa urusai. Itsumo gucha gucha bakari itte iru.*
  That guy's annoying. He never stops complaining.

gocha gocha complain; disordered

- *Nakama uchi de wa gocha gocha fuman o itte iru ga, omotedatte wa nanimo iwanai.*
  He's always expressing his dissatisfaction to his friends but he never says anything about it to anyone else.

gota gota grumble, gripe, argue; disorder, hodgepodge

- *Gota gota iu na!*
  Stop griping!

kochin sudden anger; clunk

- *Kare ga uso o tsuita to wakatta toki, atama ni kochin to kita.*
  I saw red when I realized he had lied.

121

tara tara   complain endlessly; running, dripping*

- *Kare wa shigoto ga omoshirokunai node fuhei tara tara da.*
  He moans on and on because he finds his work dull.

tsubekobe   gripe, talk too much

- *Tsubekobe iu na.*
  Shut up (and do it).
- *Tsubekobe iwazu ni.*
  Keep your mouth shut.

busu busu   mutter complaints; stab; smoldering sound

- *Kanojo ni dēto o kotowararete boku wa busu busu to hitorigoto o itta.*
  I muttered to myself after she turned me down for a date.

butsu kusa   grumble
butsu butsu   grumble, mutter; having many small holes; have a rash; simmer; chop*

- *Sono shain wa nenjū nanika butsu butsu tsubuyaite iru.*
  That employee grumbles every day of the year about one thing or another.

puri puri   be in a huff; firm flesh*
buri buri   annoyance (stronger than *puri puri*)

- *Kanojo ga ayamatta ato mo, watashi wa mada puri puri okotte ita.*
  I was still fuming even after she apologized.
- *Nan de puri puri fukurete iru no dai?*
  Why are you so angry?

pun pun   extreme annoyance; strong smell

- *Kare wa jibun ni pun pun to ikari o butsuketa.*
  He turned his fury in on himself.

musha kusha   angry, vexed, lose composure

- *Shōbai ga umaku ikanakatta node, kare wa musha kusha shite ita.*
  He was displeased because business was not going well.

musutto   sullen, not say a thing

- *Bujoku o uketa tame ni, kare wa musutto kuchi o tojite oshidamatte shimatta.*
  Because he had been insulted, he became sullen and wouldn't say a word.

muzu muzu   feel anxious or impatient; be itching to; itchy*

- *Katta mono o noro noro tsutsunde iru ten'in ni nanika iitaku natte muzu muzu shite kita.*
  I became impatient with the shop assistant who was slowly wrapping my purchase, and wanted to say something.

mutto   look angry, sulky; stifling*

- *Okāsan ga mutto shita hyōjō o shita node, kodomo wa itazura o yameta.*
  When his mother gave him an angry look, the child stopped misbehaving.

mura mura   emotion rises up

- *Akiko no iede o omoidasu tabi ni, ikari ga mura mura to komiagete kuru.*

Whenever he remembers Akiko's leaving home, burning anger wells up inside him.

Tiredness

When we are exhausted or fed up, it's good for the spirit to be able to express our feelings to others.

gakkuri   downhearted, lose spirit or energy; bent

- *Sachiko wa kyū ni gakkuri to shita.*
  Sachiko suddenly got depressed.

kusa kusa   feel depressed

- *Kimochi ga kusa kusa suru toki, chotto sake o nomeba, kimochi ga harete kuru.*
  When I'm feeling depressed, if I drink a little saké, I brighten up.

kusha kusha   depressed; crumpled, wrinkled; mumble

- *Koibito to kenka shita ato boku no kimochi ga kusha kusha shita.*
  I felt depressed after quarrelling with my girlfriend.

kuta kuta   dead tired, exhausted; fall to pieces

- *Hirō to suimin busoku de seishinteki ni mo nikutaiteki ni mo kuta kuta desu.*
  Because of overwork and lack of sleep, I'm both mentally and physically exhausted.

guttari   worn out, dead tired; wilt

- *Gorufu kōsu o hanbun mo mawattara guttari tsukarete shimatta.*
  I was worn out after going around just half the golf course.

kuyo kuyo brood, mope

- *Shiai ni makete mo kuyo kuyo suru na yo.*
  Don't mope around because you lost the match.

gunyari limp, soft, flacid; bent

- *Boku wa gunyari to ima no tatami ni suwarikonda.*
  I collapsed limply on the tatami in the living room.

gennari sick and tired, weary

- *Kachō ni monku bakari iwareta node, Keiko wa gennari shite kaette kita.*
  Keiko came back weary after the section chief chewed her out.

shio shio feel depressed, downhearted, wilted

- *Kachō ni shikararete, kare wa shio shio to jimusho o dete itta.*
  Having been scolded by his section chief, he left the office downheartedly.

shobo shobo depressed; gloomy; bleary-eyed; drizzle*

- *Kare wa warui shirase o kiite shobo shobo to kaetta.*
  He went home depressed after hearing the bad news.

shonbori miserable, disappointed, lonely

- *Shiken ni gōkaku shinakatta node, Haruko wa heya ni tojikomotte shonbori to shite ita.*

Haruko, miserable after she failed the exam, shut herself up in her room.

- *Pātii ga chūshi ni natte shimatte, kodomo wa shonbori shimashita.*
  The children were disappointed when the party was canceled.

sugo sugo   downcast, dejected, leave a place disappointed

- *Saiyō sarenakatta ōbosha wa sugo sugo to kaetta.*
  The applicants who weren't chosen left dejectedly.

hara hara   anxious, frightened; flutter soundlessly

- *Kisoku ihan ja nai ka to hara hara shite shimatta.*
  I was worried that I might be violating the rules.

heto heto   dog tired, completely exhausted

- *Fuji San ni nobotta hito-tachi wa mina heto heto datta.*
  Everyone who climbed Mount Fuji was dog tired.

hero hero   collapse; weak (baseball pitch or tennis serve)

- *Tsukarekitte mō hero hero da.*
  I'm so tired I feel like I might collapse.
- *Kara no tōkyū wa hero hero da kara, mō sukoshi renshū shinakya naranai.*
  His pitch is weak, so he must practice a bit more.

meta meta   bushed; smashed*

- *Muzukashii kōshō ni atatte, mō seishinteki ni meta meta da.*
  Having participated in the tough negotiations, I am mentally exhausted.

Sweet Dreams!

utsura utsura   doze, drowsy

- *Hikōki de no nagai tabi no aida, watashi wa utsura utsura shitsuzuketa.*
  I dozed on and off during the long flight.

uto uto   doze, nod off

- *Fuyu no densha de wa, shita kara no danbō de atatakai shi, tekitō ni yureru shi, tsui uto uto nemutte shimau.*
  On the winter trains, the heat rises from below and the train sways gently, so I inadvertently nod off.

gū gū   snoring sound; gurgle; stomach rumbles*

- *Ojiisan wa tachimachi gū gū to ōki na ibiki o kaite nemutte shimatta.*
  Grandad fell asleep in an instant, and began snoring loudly.

127

gūsuka   sound asleep; snore

* *Hiruma kara gūsuka nete ite, itsu shigoto o suru no deshō.*
  Always sound asleep during the day, when do you work?

gussuri   sound sleep (without snoring)

* *Yūbe wa gussuri nemutta node kyō wa chōshi ga saikō da.*
  I slept like a log last night, so I'm in top form today.

kokkuri, kokkuri kokkuri   nodding off; drop head (suddenly); nod in agreement

* *Obāchan wa haru no atatakai hinata de kokkuri kokkuri to inemuri shite ita.*
  Grandma kept nodding off in the warm spring sun.

torotto   sleep lightly for a short period; syrupy, glutinous; dull eyes*; melt in your mouth*

* *Chotto torotto shitara, sukkari kibun ga yoku naru.*
  If you have a little nap, I think you'll feel much better.

manjiri   not sleep a wink (used with a negative verb)

* *Yūbe wa manjiri to mo shinakatta.*
  I couldn't sleep a wink last night.

suya suya   sleep peacefully (as viewed by another person)

* *Akiko wa futon de suya suya to nemutte ita.*
  Akiko was sleeping peacefully on the futon.

·8·
GRAB BAG

There are always a few leftovers and misfits in any carefully worked-out scheme. In this chapter I've included all the phrases or examples that I couldn't bear to leave out but couldn't put anywhere else.

uttori   in a trance, in a dreamy state, entranced

* *Mankai no sakura no utsukushisa ni tada uttori to mitorete imashita.*

  I gazed at the cherry trees in full bloom, fascinated by their beauty.

uyo uyo   swarming (e.g., fish, insects)

* *Yoru no kurai daidokoro ni wa gokiburi ga uyo uyo shite iru.*

  At night, the dark kitchen is crawling with cockroaches.

uro uro   wander about, hang around

* *Kare wa yō ga nai toki de mo, jimusho no naka o uro uro shite iru.*

  He hangs around the office even when he's got nothing to do there.

kara kara   clatter; empty; laugh with a high-pitched voice; very dry*; parched*
gara gara   rattle; rough (personality); husky (voice); coarse, boisterous; almost empty; roar of thunder

* *Taifū de, yanegawara ga nanmai mo gara gara to ochite kita.*

  During the typhoon, many tiles came rattling down from the roof.

gatapishi   falling to pieces, rickety; rattle; not get along

130

- *Mō obāsan ni natte karada ga gatapishi itte iru.*
  I'm already an old lady, falling apart at the seams.

gaya gaya   clamorous

- *Shūmatsu ni naru to wakamono ga Shibuya ni atsumatte gaya gaya to sawaide iru.*
  On the weekend, young people gather noisily in Shibuya.

giko giko   sawing or grating sound

- *Kirenai nokogiri de sesse to giko giko yatte iru.*
  He is busily sawing away with a blunt saw.
- *Musume no hiku baiorin no giko giko iu oto wa mimizawari da.*
  The grating sound of my daughter's violin playing is hard on the ears.

gikushaku   things don't go well; jerky

- *Taijin kankei ga gikushaku shite kuru to monogoto ga maruku osamaranai.*
  When personal relations become strained, it is difficult to patch things up.

giza giza   jagged, serrated

- *Kono ki no ha wa fuchi ga giza giza shite iru.*
  The leaves of this tree have serrated edges.

kibi kibi   lively, brisk

- *Inaka no kodomo wa tokai no kodomo yori kibi kibi shite iru.*
  Children who live in the country are livelier than city kids.

kukutto   chuckle; jerk (e.g., on a fishing line)
kukku   stifled giggle

- *Tsuri o shite ite, kukutto atari ga kita node, awatete tsuri zao o ageta.*
  While I was fishing, I felt the line jerk and quickly pulled up my rod.

kukkiri   stand out clearly, distinctly

- *Dorobō no ashiato ga mado no shita no tsuchi ni kukkiri to mieta.*
  The robber's footprint stood out clearly in the soil under the window.

jitabata   panic, writhe, thrash about

- *Jishin ga okorihajimeta toki, shain wa minna jitabata shitari shinakatta.*
  When the earthquake started, the employees didn't panic.

jikkuri   think carefully; talk things over; carefully*

- *Dono shigoto o shitai ka? Jikkuri kangaete mite kudasai.*
  What kind of work do you want to do? Try to think about it very carefully.
- *Jugyō ga sunde kara jikkuri hanashiaimashō.*
  Let's talk things over after school.

yukkuri   slowly, in a relaxed manner, by easy stages

- *Yama no chōjō made yukkuri jikan o kakete nobotta node kaerimichi wa kyanpujō made isoide modorimashita.*
  Having taken our time climbing to the top of the mountain, we hurried back to the campsite.
- *Go-yukkuri dōzo.*
  Please make yourself at home.

sosokusa   rush; hurried and incomplete

- *Meiko wa uchi e kaeru to, sosokusa to nedoko ni haitte nemutte shimatta.*
  Meiko came home, hurried into bed and fell asleep.

sotto   gently; alone; do something quietly; in secret

- *Itaria de katta kōka na gurasu o kowasanai yō ni sotto araimashita.*
  She gently washed the expensive glasses she bought in Italy so as not to break them.

- *Sotto shite oite kure.*
  Leave me alone.

sokkuri   look alike; the whole of something

- *Ano futari no obāsan wa sokkuri da. Futago ni chigai nai.*
  Those two grannies look exactly the same. They must be twins.

chiguhagu   out of harmony, not match; haywire, disorganized*

- *Sachiko no setsumei wa chiguhagu de wakaranakatta.*
  Sachiko's explanation was incoherent and I couldn't understand it.
- *Ano jaketto to sukāto wa dōmo chiguhagu na kanji ga suru.*
  Somehow that skirt and jacket don't seem to go together.

choki choki   snip snip (of scissors)

- *Atsuko wa hasami de yōfuku no kiji o choki choki to kitte ita.*
  Atsuko was snipping away at the cloth with her scissors.

choko choko   waddle, toddle; finish quickly; often

- *Watashi no kodomo wa jikkagetsu kara choko choko arukihajimeta.*
  My child began toddling from the age of ten months.
- *Choko choko to kantan ni shigoto o sumasete, uchi e kaerō.*
  Let's finish up the work quickly and go home.

chon chon   two written dots; repeated sound of wooden clappers

  Chon on its own can be used to mean a comma or a stop.

- *"Ha" ni chon chon o uteba, "ba" ni naru.*
  Put two dots on *ha* and it becomes *ba*.

dotabata   romp (children), racket; slapstick

- *Kodomo-tachi ga ichinichijū uchi no naka de dotabata shita node, atama ga itaku natta.*
  Because the children were romping about the house all day, I have a headache.

donpishari   perfectly in order, dead on

- *Sono yakugara wa kanojo ni donpishari ni atte iru.*
  That role fits her perfectly.
- *Chōjiri ga ippen de donpishari to atte ii kibun datta.*
  I felt great when the accounts balanced perfectly the first time.

noro noro   extremely slow movement

- *Saijitsu ni Hakone kara kaetta toki, Tōmei kōsoku dōro wa gojikkiro no jūtai de Tōkyō made noro noro unten datta.*
  When we came back from Hakone on the national holiday, there was a fifty-kilometer long traffic jam on the Tomei Expressway going all the way to Tokyo.

pachikuri   blink in surprise

- *Gaikokujin wa Nihon no gyūniku no nedan ni me o pachi-kuri saseru bakari da.*
  Foreigners can do nothing but blink in surprise at the price of Japanese beef.

hakkiri   clearly, plainly, distinctly, correctly

- *Hakkiri to hanashite kudasai.*
  Please speak clearly.

bisshiri   packed

- *Tsūkin ressha wa itsumo sarariiman to ōeru de bisshiri da.*
  The commuter train is always packed with office workers.

buka buka   baggy; blow a brass instrument

- *Kono surakkusu wa o-shiri no tokoro ga buka buka shite iru.*
  The seat of these slacks is baggy.

puka puka   puff; smoke many cigarettes; blow a harmonica; float up

- *Kare wa ichinichijū puka puka tabako o fukashite iru.*
  He puffs away on cigarettes all day long.

hera hera   laugh (when embarrassed)
bera bera   blab on and on, chatter; cheap and thin (e.g., cloth)
pera pera   fluent; speak frivolously; turn page; cheap and thin (e.g., cloth)

- *Kare wa uso ga wakatta toki, hera hera to waratta.*
  When his lie was discovered, he laughed embarrassedly.
- *Kanojo wa asa kara ban made tonari no obasan to bera bera shaberimasu.*
  She blabs on and on all day with the woman next door.
- *Ano hito wa Furansugo ga pera pera da ne.*
  His French is fluent.

I'm told there is an English school that says in their advertisement, *"Kotoshi hera hera. Rainen pera pera!"* "This year all I can do is laugh embarrassedly (because I can't speak English). Next year I will be fluent!" It's a catchy jingle, anyway.

hoi hoi   rashly, easily; without any trouble

- *Ano hito wa shitashii yūjin da kara nan de mo hoi hoi to hikiukete kureru yo.*
  He's a close friend of mine. He'll straighten things out for you in no time.

pokari   hit once; wide open, gape; float, pop up

- *Kurai tokoro o aruite iru to, ikinari ushiro kara bō no yō na mono de pokari to nagurareta.*
  While walking in a dark place, I was suddenly hit from behind with some kind of stick.
- *Aki no aozora ni shiroi kumo ga pokari to ukande iru.*
  A white cloud is floating in the blue autumn sky.

hotto   sigh (of relief)

- *Shiken ga yōyaku owatta node, watashi wa hotto shita.*
  I breathed a sigh of relief when the exams were finally over.

potsun   alone, isolated; sound of a single drop hitting something

- *Gakusei jidai no totemo nakayoku shite ita tomodachi to wa sotsugyō go potsun to renraku ga todaeta.*
  Although we were very good friends during our student days, I haven't heard anything from him since we graduated.

bon'yari   indistinct, blurred; absentminded; loaf about*

- *Fuji San ga bon'yari to tōku ni kasunde ita.*
  Mount Fuji was dimly visible in the distance.

waku waku   excitedly; anxiously

- *Kaigai ryokō no keikaku o tatenagara mune ga waku waku shita.*
  I felt excited while I was planning my trip abroad.

And to end on a happy note:

niko niko   smile warmly, grin; laugh

- *Akachan wa genki ni niko niko to waratte iru.*
  The baby is in good spirits and smiling happily.

· LISTING OF ENTRIES ·

139

boso boso   stale; mumble   59
bosotto   stale; mumble; unsociable   59
bota bota   continuous dripping   38
bote bote   grossly fat   97
botteri   large, fat, fleshy, heavy   96
bū bū   blow a horn, toot; human griping about something; pig's grunt or snort   23, 102
buka buka   baggy; blow a brass instrument   136
buku buku   sound of bubbling; swish fluid in one's mouth; swollen and fat   49, 96
būn, bun bun   buzz of a bee or horsefly   27
bura bura   waste time, idle; dangle   68
buri buri   annoyance (stronger than *puri puri*)   122
busu busu   mutter complaints; stab; smoldering sound   122
butsu butsu   chop; simmer; having many small holes; have a rash; mutter, grumble   49, 122
butsu kusa   grumble   122
byū byū   whistle (stronger than *hyū hyū*)   42

chakkari   shrewd, cunning; having sound business sense   66
chanto   do properly, correctly, exactly; perfectly   66
chara chara   dress up too much; flirt; jangle; flatter; sexy; overdone finery   94
chibi chibi   small sips; nibble; little by little   82
chiguhagu   disharmony, not match; haywire, disorganized   66, 134
chiin chiin   ding dong   102
chika chika   flicker (of stars), flash (of lights); irritated (eyes)   44
chima chima   fine, pinched features; neatly   94
chin chin   ding ding; kettle whistling; (dog) stands up   102
chinchirorin   cricket's chirp   26
chira chira   twinkling of stars; flickering light; occasional glimpses; fluttering of snow or falling blossoms   37, 44
chiri chiri   crinkly; frizzy; jingle, continual small ring; shrink in fear   94
chirin chirin   tinkle, jingle, jangle (louder than *chiri chiri,* with pauses between sounds)   102
chiyahoya   butter someone up, curry favor   66
choki choki   snip snip (of scissors)   134
choko choko   waddle, toddle; finish quickly; often   134
chon chon   two written dots; repeated sound of wooden clappers   134

gabo gabo   rake in money; loose-fitting; gurgling sound   72, 81
gabotto   large profit, large loss   73
gabu gabu   gulp, guzzle   81
gakkuri   downhearted, lose spirit or energy; bent   124
gami gami   nagging   88
gan gan   do something vigorously; dull heavy clang; throbbing
   headache   101, 110, 116
gappo gappo   rake in money   72
gappori   rake in money in one go, or lose it all at once   72
gappuri   lock together   109
gara gara   rattle; rough (personality); husky (voice); coarse, boisterous;
   almost empty; roar of thunder   130
gari gari   rock hard; scratching; thin; obsessed   54
gasa gasa   rough, insensitive; noisy, rustle; dried out   87
gashitto   strongly built   107
gasshiri   very solidly built, massive   107
gata gata   be shaky; tremble; rattle; sudden decline; complain   76,
   120
gatapishi   falling to pieces, rickety; rattle; not get along   130
gatchiri   firmly, solidly; carefully do something; careful with
   money   72, 109
gatsu gatsu   greedy, hungry   50
gatsun   bang   110
gatto   seize, hold with strength   109
gaya gaya   clamorous   131
gē gē   retch, vomit   84
gennari   sick and tired, weary   125
gero gero   vomit continuously   84
gessori   look emaciated, haggard   117
giko giko   sawing or grating sound   131
gikushaku   things don't go well; jerky   132
gikutto   suddenly hurt (one's back); be startled   117
gira gira   intense glaring sunlight; dazzling light (like *kira kira* but
   stronger)   38
giri giri   just in time or within the limit; rock bottom price; grating,
   grinding   74
gisu gisu   very thin; cold (personality or atmosphere)   92
giza giza   jagged, serrated   132
gocha gocha   complain; disordered   121
gochi gochi   rock hard (harder than *kochi kochi*)   55
gohon gohon   cough loudly   117

goku goku   gulping sound in throat, glug glug   82
gon   bang (heads); ring   111
gori gori   hard, rough; crunch (chewing on a hard object like a bone); scratch   55
goro goro   purr; laze about; lumpy; roll, rumble   21, 42
gorori   (heavy object) rolling; lying awkwardly   111
gossori   robbed clean; entirely, completely   74
gota gota   grumble, gripe, argue; disorder, hodgepodge   121
gote gote   gaudy; thick and heavy; say over and over again   92
goto goto   boil vigorously, heavy rattle   47
gotsu gotsu   rough or durable (body type); sound of two hard things banging into one another   92
gū gū   snoring sound; gurgle; stomach rumbles   50, 127
gubiri gubiri   guzzle   82
gucha gucha   complain; messy; chew, suck; mushy and wet   54, 121
guden guden   get drunk (and not remember)   85
gui gui   push or pull with all one's strength; drink vigorously, gulp   81, 110
guitto   apply all one's strength at once; gulp down in one go   81, 110
gun   put strength into a single effort; striking progress   73, 110
gun gun   vigorous, striking progress   73
gunya gunya   soft and weak   98
gunyari   limp, soft, flacid; bent   125
gura gura   boil; fickle; tremor; rickety; loose   47, 117
gusha gusha   squashed and runny, splat, crumple; messy; ruin   54
gusho gusho   soaking wet, sopping wet   30
gusshori   drenched   31
gussuri   sound sleep (without snoring)   128
gūsuka   sound asleep; snore   128
gutsu gutsu   simmer, boil   47
guttari   worn out, dead tired; wilt   124
gutto   gulp; concentrated action; feel strongly; pull forcefully   82
guzu guzu   make slow progress, dillydally; sniffle; complain   68, 121
gyutto   push or squeeze with force   110

hakkiri   clearly, plainly, distinctly, correctly   136
hara hara   anxious, frightened; flutter soundlessly   126
hera hera   laugh (when embarrassed)   136
hero hero   collapse; weak (baseball pitch or tennis serve)   126
heto heto   dog tired, completely exhausted   126
hii hii   scream in pain   118

hin hin neigh 23
hin'yari cool 37
hiri hiri piquant 58
hita hita thin covering of water; lapping water (on the side of a boat); approach gradually 49
hiya hiya feel cold continuously; shudder; feel nervous or frightened 36
hiyari shudder due to cold, feel a sudden chill; momentarily panic-striken 36
hiyatto suddenly feel cold or very frightened 36
hō, hō hō owl's hooting 26
hō hokekyo nightingale's song 26
hoi hoi rashly, easily; without any trouble 137
hoka hoka nicely steaming, hot food; feel warm and pleasant 59
hoku hoku soft and tasty (baked, starchy food); pleased, beaming 59
horotto nice bitter taste; slight stimulation of the senses; feel pleasure or sympathy; something light and small falling (e.g., a tear); tipsy 60, 83
hotto sigh (of relief) 137
hoya hoya food hot from the oven; fresh state (for both people and things) 60, 100
hyū hyū whistle; asthmatic wheeze 42

icha icha showing affection in public 98
iji iji introverted, inhibited 87
ira ira irritated, on edge 120
iso iso light-hearted and cheerful; looking forward to something, eager 87

jā jā sizzle (in oil); pour, hose down 48
jabu jabu stir strongly; splash about 48
jan jan sell like hot cakes; lavish money on; receive lots of money; things occurring one after another; ring 74
jara jara overdone finery; clatter, jangle 93
jii jii sound of something burning; cicada's chirp 22, 47
jikkuri carefully; talk things over; think carefully 111, 133
jime jime melancholy, depressed; dark, gloomy; damp 32, 90
jin, jiin pins and needles; feel like you are going to cry; ringing vibration; numbing cold 37, 118
jiri jiri sizzle; ring; fierce sunlight; little by little, gradually 48

jitabata   panic; writhe, thrash about   132
jito jito   clammy, feel sticky with dampness   32
jittori   moist with sweat   31
jū jū   hiss, sizzle   48

kā kā   caw caw   22
kachi kachi   stubborn; hard; ticking; click-clack of wooden clappers   88
kakka   burn with rage; blush; hot sensation; continuous heat or light   38, 120
kakkō   cuckoo's song   25
kan kan   very angry; clang, high clear ring; blazing sun or heat   38, 101, 121
kara kara   parched; empty; laugh with a high-pitched voice; clatter; very dry   40, 81, 130
karappo   empty   76
karari   crisp; clatter; dry, clear; cheerful   40, 47, 89
karatto   crisp; weather clears up   40, 54
kari kari   crisp, crunchy; worked up   54, 120
kasu kasu   dry; just barely reach a standard level (lifestyle) or deadline   54
katto   fly into a rage; thump, bang; sudden heat or light   120
keba keba   lavish, heavy, gaudy   92
kero kero   frog's croaking   26
kibi kibi   lively, brisk   132
kichi kichi   do something just so; tight schedule   63
kichin   smart, stylish, organized   92
kira kira   twinkle, glitter, shine   43
kiri kiri   so busy you seem to be spinning; sharp continuous pain   64, 117
kitchiri   tight schedule; exact; well-fitting; tight (cork)   63
kochi kochi   inflexible, stubborn; tense; rock hard   55, 89
kochin   sudden anger; clunk   121
kokekokkō   cock-a-doodle-doo   24
kokkuri, kokkuri kokkuri   nodding off; drop head (suddenly); nod in agreement   128
kokun   gulp down; drop head suddenly (e.g., when falling asleep)   82
kon kon   fox's yelp; snow falling for a long time; light knocking or coughing   25
kongari   nicely browned, tan   55
kori kori   rubbery; stiff (shoulders); firm muscle   55, 107

koro koro plump; ring of a bell; rolling; giggling; cricket's chirp 26, 93
kose kose fussy; narrow, cramped 89
kossori do something in secret 64
kote kote smother; rich food; paint (makeup) on thick 55
koto koto simmer, boil lightly, rattle 47
kotsu kotsu work at over a long period; sound of hard shoes clicking on the pavement; knocking or rapping sound 64
kotteri rich, heavy food; smothered in; paint (makeup) on thick 55
kucha kucha chewing sound; crumple 50
kukkiri stand out clearly, distinctly 132
kukku stifled giggle 132
kukū drink in one gulp 82
kukutto chuckle; jerk (e.g., on a fishing line) 132
kunya kunya bend easily, irresolute 89
kura kura boil; feel dizzy 47
kusa kusa feel depressed 124
kusha kusha depressed; crumpled, wrinkled; mumble 124
kuta kuta dead tired, exhausted; fall to pieces 124
kuyo kuyo brood, mope 125
kyakkya monkey's shriek 25
kyan kyan yap, yelp of a dog in pain, yip yap of a small dog 20
kyoto kyoto jittery, look around nervously 89
kyū kyū hard up for money; tight (schedule); squeaky (shoes) 77
kyutto gulp; tight; pinch 81

mago mago hang around; confused 69
manjiri not sleep a wink 128
mecha kucha incoherent; confused, messy; preposterous; destroyed 69
mecha mecha all screwed up, disorderly; logically inconsistent; in a mess 69
mē mē goat's or sheep's bleat 23
meki meki make marked progress; sell like hot cakes 75
mero mero drunk; discouraged; controlled by one's wife 85
meta meta smashed; bushed 85, 126
miin miin cicada's chirp 22
mitchiri hard training 114
mō mō moo 24
mogu mogu chew softly; mumble 53
moji moji fidget; hesitatingly 91

pari pari   devoted; stiff (collar); eager; new; chew vigorously   51, 67

paritto   crisp; fresh and new   58

pasa pasa   dry, stale; flutter   58

patto   vivid lively state (but used negatively to mean dull); sudden rapid action; scatter   113

peko peko   ravenously hungry; kowtow   51, 68

pen pen   pluck a samisen   103

pera pera   fluent; speak frivolously; turn page; cheap and thin (e.g., cloth)   136

pero pero   lick, poke tongue out repeatedly   52

perori   eat up (not as brief as *perotto*); lick quickly; stick out one's tongue   52

perotto   swallow in one mouthful, eat a lot in a very short time   52

pii hyororo   hawk's cry; sound of a flute   26

pii pii   in dire straits (financially); a high-pitched sound; chirp   77

pika pika   stars shine brightly; brand new   43

pikatto   flash of lightning   43

pin pin   healthy; twang; strained; pull hard   119

piri piri   spicy food (more spicy than *hiri hiri*); blow a whistle; rip; nervous; prickling pain   58, 119

piritto   sharpness, freshness   108

piyo piyo   cheep cheep   24

pocha pocha   chubby and cute; roly-poly   96

pokari   hit once; wide open, gape; float, pop up   137

pokkari   float up; suddenly appear; open wide   41

pokkuri   suddenly die; fragile   119

pon   pull out a cork; without hesitation, casually; pat   83

pon pon   sell like hot cakes; in rapid succession; clap hands; speak without reserve; popping corks   75, 83

poppo   pigeon's coo   21

pori pori   crunch, munch; scratch (lighter sound than *bori bori*)   52

poro poro   dry and crumbly; (tears) fall one after another   60

poron poron   pluck or strum a stringed instrument (e.g., a guitar or a harp); strike piano keys   103

pota pota   continuous dripping (lighter sound than *bota bota*), plop plop   38

potchari   nicely plump, chubby and cute; splash   96

potsun   alone, isolated; sound of a single drop hitting something   137

pū pū   blow a horn (a higher pitched sound than *bū bū*)   102

puka puka   puff; smoke many cigarettes; blow a harmonica; float up   136

pun pun   extreme annoyance; strong smell   123
puri puri   be in a huff; firm flesh   58, 122
putsutto, putsun   sound of a tense object being cut or broken; prick, pierce   114
pyū pyū   shrill whistle   42

rin rin   chirp of the *suzumushi* (bush cricket); ringing sound   22
rō rō   singing or reciting in a loud, clear voice   103

saba saba   carefree, detached; fresh, neat; feel relieved   90
saku saku   cut (a crisp vegetable); crunch (while eating or walking on snow)   47
sappari   refreshing; not at all; open, fresh and simple   55, 89
sarari   easygoing, carefree; smooth action, slide; fresh and dry   41, 90
seka seka   busily, unsettled, rushing, busybody   65
sesse   busily, work hard   66
shā shā   brazen; shower, spray   90
shaki shaki   crisp (fruit or vegetables); brisk   56, 64
shakitto   fresh and crisp (in mouth or to touch); a fresh feeling   56
shanari shanari   gracefully; haughtily   93
shari shari   crisp, tangy, fresh; scrape   56
shikkari   steady, responsible, firm; sufficient   90
shikkuri   get along well (usually used in the negative sense)   98
shiko shiko   pleasantly firm texture (in mouth)   56
shiku shiku   dull pain; sob, cry (softly)   117
shin, shiin   utterly quiet   44
shin shin   snow falls thick and fast   37
shinnari   soft, flexible   48
shio shio   feel depressed, downhearted, wilted   125
shippori   (affectionate lovers get) thoroughly soaked (in the rain)   32
shito shito   drizzle; feel damp   32
shittori   moist; pleasantly calm and elegant, placid, quiet, tranquil   31, 90
shobo shobo   depressed; gloomy; bleary-eyed; drizzle   32, 125
shonbori   miserable, disappointed, lonely   125
sokkuri   look alike; the whole of something   134
soro soro   slow, gradual progress; about time to   74
sosokusa   rush; hurried and incomplete   133
sotto   gently; alone; do something quietly; in secret   133
soyo soyo   light breeze   42

sū sū   a draft; sound of nasal breathing   35
sugo sugo   downcast, dejected, leave a place disappointed   126
sukatto   fresh, clean; clear   56
sukkiri   simple, perky; trim; refreshing   94
sunnari   slender; progress without a hitch   73, 94
sura sura   proceed smoothly, without a hitch; flow   73
surari   long and slender; smooth unbroken movement, nimbly   94
suru suru   slurp; move smoothly   50
suten, sutten   tumble and fall   111
suttenten   flat broke   76
suya suya   sleep peacefully (as viewed by another person)   128

taji taji   be thrown off balance; cannot hold one's own   66, 112
tappuri   full, oodles, plenty   50
tara tara   running, dripping; complain endlessly   48, 122
teka teka   shiny, brightly   95
toge toge   harsh, prickly, thorny; sarcastic   91
toku toku   sound or act of pouring a liquid; speak proudly   83
ton ton   be on par (e.g., a balance of revenue and expenditure); proceed smoothly; tapping, knocking   76
toppuri   night deepens; pleasantly steeped in   33, 43
toro toro   melted; weak fire; doze off   57
torotto   melt in your mouth; glutinous, syrupy; dull eyes; sleep lightly for a short period   51, 118, 128
tsubekobe   gripe, talk too much   122
tsuke tsuke   blunt, speak one's mind without hesitation   67
tsun, tsūn   stinging, pungent (e.g., ammonia or vinegar); pointed; standoffish   56, 90
tsuru tsuru   slurp vigorously; slippery; smooth; bald   50

uji uji   wishy-washy, indecisive   87
uka uka   dream away one's time; lack direction or a plan; careless; settled   68
uki uki   eager, light-hearted, cheerful   87
ukkari   inadvertently, carelessly, thoughtlessly   68
un un   groan (with effort or pain); nod (in agreement)   114
unzari   fed up, sick and tired   63
uro uro   wander about, hang around   130
uto uto   doze, nod off   127
utsura utsura   doze, drowsy   127
uttori   in a trance, in a dreamy state, entranced   130

uyo uyo   swarming (*e.g.*, fish, insects)   130

waku waku   excitedly; anxiously   138
wan wan   woof woof, bowwow   20

yakimoki   anxious, on edge; impatient   70
yore yore   wrinkled or worn-out clothing   97
yoro yoro   stagger; lose one's balance   84, 114
yukkuri   slowly, in a relaxed manner, by easy stages   133
yura yura   (image) wavers (in the hot air)   40
yuttari   mellow, carefree; leisurely; spacious   97

zā zā   sound of a downpour, sound of a lot of water flowing (e.g., a
  waterfall)   31
zaku zaku   money rolls in; rough weave; crunch   74
zatto, zātto   sound of a sudden downpour; roughly, approximately   31
zawa zawa   chilly; rustling sound; clamor of a crowd   35
zokkon   deeply involved, crazy about   99
zoku zoku   shiver due to the cold; shiver with excitement or pleasure;
  shiver in fear; things happen one after another   35
zotto   a cold shiver down one's spine   35
zuba zuba   straight-talking; directly   65
zuke zuke   blunt, speak one's mind without hesitation (in a more
  direct way than *tsuke tsuke*)   67
zuki zuki   heartache; continual painful throb   99, 118
zukin   one sharp pain; feel a sharp pang of guilt   118
zukin zukin   continual throbbing pain (heavier than *zuki
  zuki*)   118
zun zun   rapid progress or regression   73
zunguri   short and fat   94
zuru zuru   slowly slip backward; sound of a heavy object being
  dragged; lose repeatedly; slurp   50, 111
zuta zuta   heartbroken; cut in ribbons, shredded   99